William Judah Thomson

Te Pito te Henua

Or, Easter Island

William Judah Thomson

Te Pito te Henua
Or, Easter Island

ISBN/EAN: 9783741182969

Manufactured in Europe, USA, Canada, Australia, Japa

Cover: Foto ©Andreas Hilbeck / pixelio.de

Manufactured and distributed by brebook publishing software (www.brebook.com)

William Judah Thomson

Te Pito te Henua

SMITHSONIAN INSTITUTION.
UNITED STATES NATIONAL MUSEUM.

TE PITO TE HENUA, OR EASTER ISLAND

BY

WILLIAM J. THOMSON,
Paymaster, U. S. Navy.

From the Report of the National Museum, 1888-'89, pages 447-552 (with plates XII-LX).

WASHINGTON:
GOVERNMENT PRINTING OFFICE.
1891.

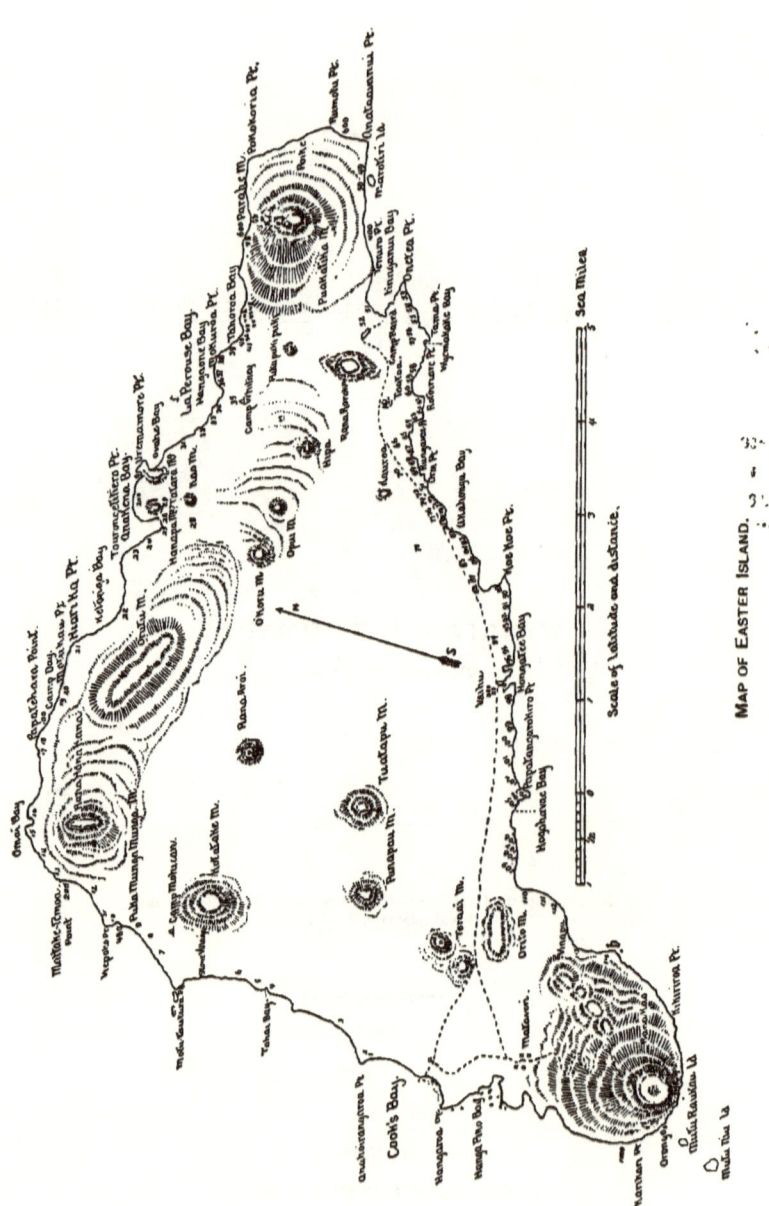

MAP OF EASTER ISLAND.

TE PITO TE HENUA, OR EASTER ISLAND.

By Paymaster WILLIAM J. THOMSON, U. S. Navy.

THE DISCOVERY OF EASTER ISLAND.

The honor of the discovery of Easter Island is contested by several of the earlier voyagers in the Pacific. Spanish writers claim that the island was sighted by Mendana in 1566, but the account is by no means authenticated, and the records preserved are not sufficiently accurate to determine the exact track sailed over by that ancient mariner. Captain Davis is credited by Capt. William Dampier with being the first to sight the island, and Lionel Wafer, who cruised with that bold navigator, on board of the *Batchelor's Delight*, gives the following account of the discovery in the year 1687:

Bound to the southward, in latitude 12 degrees 30 minutes and about 150 leagues off the coast, experienced a shock of earthquake, that was afterwards found to correspond with the destruction of Callao by earthquake. Having recovered from our fright we kept on to the southward. We steered south-and-by-east-half-easterly, until we came to latitude 27 degrees 20 minutes south, when about two hours before day we fell in with a small low, sandy island and heard a great roaring noise, like that of the sea beating upon the shore, right ahead of the ship. Whereupon the sailors, fearing to fall foul upon the shore before day, desired the captain to put the ship about, and to stand off until the day appeared; to which the captain gave his consent. So we plied off till day and then stood in again with the land, which proved to be a small flat island, without any guard of rocks. We stood in within a quarter of a mile of the shore and could see it plainly, for it was a clear morning, not foggy or hazy. To the westward about 12 leagues, by judgment, we saw a range of high land, which we took to be islands, for there were several partitions in the prospect.

This land seemed to reach about 14 or 16 leagues in a range, and there came great flocks of fowls. I and many more of our men would have made this land and have gone ashore on it, but the captain would not permit us. The small island bears from Copiapó almost due east 500 leagues, and from the Galapagos, under the line, 600 leagues.

Unfortunately, none of the voyagers on board of the *Batchelor's Delight* were permitted to land upon this unknown island, nor is mention made in the narratives of monoliths or unusual structures that might have been observed from the short distance in which it is claimed they approached the shore. The apparent inaccuracy in the description of the appearance of the land may have been due to the peculiar bearing of the vessel, but it gives foundation to the claim of Admiral Roggeveen, that Davis's island was not identical with the one discovered by him on April 7, 1722, and named Easter Island in commemoration of the day upon which the land was sighted. Roggeveen says:

When we approached nearer the land we saw distinctly from a short distance that the description of the sandy and low island did not accord in the least with our discovery. Furthermore, it could not be the same land which the aforesaid voyagers claim to have seen stretching 14 to 16 leagues in front of them, and near the highland which Dampier judged to be the coast-line of the unknown south. That Easter Island can not be the sandy island described by Davis is clear, because that was small and low, while on the contrary Easter Island is high and towers above the sea, having also two elevations rising above the level part. It would not be possible to mistake, even at the dry season of the year, the grass and verdure that covers the hill-sides for barren sand. After the Dutch custom of the day, the admiral assembled the commanders of the three vessels composing his fleet—the *Arend*, the *African Galley*, and the *Thienhoven*—in council to pass formal resolutions claiming the discovery of the land. The proceedings of the assembly state that on Easter day land was sighted about 9 miles distant, of moderate height, and containing an area of about 6 Dutch miles. The weather being calm the vessels were not able to secure an anchorage near the land until the next day. The island was found to be destitute of trees, but with a fertile soil producing bananas, potatoes, and sugar-cane of extraordinary thickness. It was unanimously agreed that both from the difference in the location as well as the appearance of the land seen by Davis, the fact was established beyond doubt that the island just discovered could not be the same. These proceedings, being drawn up, were formally signed by Jacob Roggeveen, Jan Koster, Cornelius Bonman, and Roelof Rosendaal. After sailing from Easter Island the vessels spent a number of days in a search for the low sandy island described by Davis, but not with success.

The unreliable Behrens mentions in the "Two Years' Voyage" the discovery of Easter Island by Roggeveen on the day celebrated as the resurrection of the Lord (April 6, 1722), in latitude 27 degrees south and longitude 268 degrees west.

Capt. F. W. Beechey, R. N., commanding H. M. S. *Blossom* (November, 1825), referring to the discovery of Easter Island, finds the credit due to Davis, giving the following reasons for the conclusions drawn:

Had such an island been in existence answering to the description of that seen by Davis, geographers would not have been long in reconciling their opinions on the subject of his discovery, as in all probability they would have waived their objections to its distance from Copiapó in consideration of its identity. The subject of the supposed discovery has been often discussed; and when the data are so unsatisfactory as to allow one party to choose the islands of Felix and Ambrose for the land in question, and the other Easter Island, two places nearly 1,600 miles apart, they are not likely to be speedily reconciled unless two islands exactly answering the description given by Davis, and situated in the proper latitude, shall be found.

Without entering upon a question which presents so many difficulties, I shall merely observe that, considering the rapid current that exists in the vicinity of the Galapagos, and extends, though with diminished force, throughout the trade-wind, the error in Davis's reckoning is not more than might have happened to any dull sailing vessel circumstanced as he was. In a short run from Juan Fernandez to Easter Island, Behrens, who was with Roggeveen, was drifted 318 geographical miles to the westward of his supposed situation. H. M. S. *Blossom* in passing over the same ground experienced a set of 270 miles in the short space of 18 days. M. La Pérouse on his arrival at Sandwich Islands from Concepcion, touching at Easter Island on his way, found a similar error of 300 miles in the course of that passage. It is fair to presume that Davis was longer in crossing from the Galapagos to Easter Island than either of those vessels or, at least, than the *Blossom*; and it is consequently but reasonable to allow him a greater error. particularly as the first part of his route was through a much stronger current. But taking the error in the *Blossom's* reckoning as a fair amount, and applying it to the distance given by Wafer, there will remain only 204 miles unaccounted for between it and the real position of Easter Island, which, from the foregoing considerations, added to the manner in which reckonings were formerly kept, does not appear to me to exceed the limit that might reasonably be ascribed to those causes.

M. La Pérouse was of the opinion that the islands of Felix and Ambrose were those under discussion, and in order to reconcile their distance from Capiapó with that given by Wafer, has imputed to him a mistake of a figure in his text, without considering that it would have been next to impossible for Davis to have pursued a direct course from the Galapagos to those islands (especially at the season in which his voyage was made), but on the contrary that he would be compelled to make a circuit which would have brought him much nearer to Easter Island, and that Davis acquainted Dampier with the situation of his discovery, which agreed with that contained in Wafer's account.

The alteration of a figure, it must be admitted, is rather arbitrary, as it has nothing to support it but the circumstance of the number of islands being the same. A mistake certainly might have occurred, but in the admission of it either party may claim it as an advantage by interpreting the presumed error in a way which would support his own opinion.

Cook and Pérouse differ in a very trifling degree from each other, and also from us, in the geographical position of Easter Island. The longitude is, by Cook, 109 degrees 46 minutes 20 seconds, and deducting 18 minutes 30 seconds, in consequence of certain corrections made at Fetegu Island, leaves 109 degrees, 27 minutes, 50 seconds west. That by Pérouse, allowing the longitude of Concepcion to be 72 degrees 56 minutes 30 seconds west, is 109 degrees 32 minutes 10 seconds west, and our own is 109 degrees 24 minutes 54 seconds west.

Admitting that the land was first sighted by Davis, the fact is beyond question that the Dutchmen under Roggeveen were the first Europeans to land on the island. From the unfortunate termination of his cruise, and the suppression of his official journal for so many years, but little has been handed down to us in the way of description of the island as it then appeared.

The Spaniards sighted the island in 1770, and gave it the name of St. Carlos. Captain Cook called it Easter Island in March, 1774, and sent an expedition on shore, but his log affords little in regard to its general appearance beyond the fact that it was parched and desolate, and of no value as a place of refreshment.

M. Bernizet, geographical engineer, who visited the island in April, 1786, with the La Pérouse expedition, describes its appearance with care, and after the lapse of a century his notes are found to be sufficiently accurate for ordinary purposes.

Amasa Delano, Kotzebue, Lisiansky, and many other voyagers made brief calls at the island, and their journals afford little information. The recent French, Spanish, and English charts are sufficiently accurate in the main features, but some of the coast lines were evidently established from running surveys, and are incorrect. During the stay of the

Mohican Lieut. F. M. Symonds, with Naval Cadet C. M. McCormick as assistant, made a careful survey of the island, and their chart, herewith appended, will be found accurate and replete with interest. (Plate XII.)

SAILING DIRECTIONS.

Vessels anchoring on this unprotected coast must be guided entirely by the direction of the wind at the time. The *Mohican* anchored in the roadstead of Hanga Roa (Cook's Bay on the English charts) on the morning of December 19, 1886, and afterwards moved to a position off Anakena Bay (La Pérouse Bay), for convenience in shipping the stone image, now in the National Museum.

On the south coast there are good anchorages during northerly and westerly winds, but there is usually a heavy swell from the southwest, making the boat-landings at Vaihu both difficult and dangerous. With easterly winds a good anchorage will be found just outside of Hanga Pico Bay, with sandy bottom, in about 26 fathoms of water, and the boat-landing will be found safe. The best boat-landing on the island is at Anakena Bay; the beach is comparatively free from stones, and even with northerly winds the landing would be no more difficult than is usual at Funchal.

The rise and fall of the tide at Easter Island is about 2 feet. The northerly and westerly winds do not produce a high sea, but generally bring rain, and are usually confined to the winter season. These winds are known to the natives as "papakino" (ill-force). The northeast wind is called "tongariki;" it is variable, and frequent in summer. The southeast wind, known as "anoraro" (wide expanse), is the prevailing wind in summer. The south wind, called "motu-rauri" (dark leaf rock), blows in winter. The southwest wind blows strong in winter, and brings rain and a high sea. Vaitara (cut-water) is a winter wind from the west. The prevailing winds are from an easterly direction, and all others are of short duration. Light airs that frequently shift direction are usually accompanied by rain, and are called by the natives "tepuhanga" (blows drift on shore), the reason for which is obvious.

GEOLOGICAL FEATURES.

The geological features of the island are replete with interest. The formation is purely of a volcanic character and embraces every variety pertaining to that structure. Basaltic, cellular, and tufaceous lavas abound in diversified forms. The basaltic is generally porous and scoriform, but on the slope of the hills the substrata are frequently as compact and dense as that of the coast-line. Near Anakena may be seen hills composed of scoria quite as cellular as pumice, and in close proximity compact beds having a dark blue basis, composed of crystals of glassy feldspar and olivine.

The cellular formation is mixed pumice and slag, in some cases similar to volcanic cinder, having the lightness and qualities of coke. In some of the varieties the cavities are filled with olivine crystals partly decomposed, but generally the cavities are empty. This lava when mixed with feldspar is sometimes of gray color; not unfrequently several tints of red may be seen, though the most common is a dark, lusterless brown.

The tufaceous lavas are extremely interesting, because they form the most prominent feature in the physiognomy of the island. To this geological structure, with the incessant action of the trade-winds and heavy rains, is due the fact that the island is surrounded by precipitous cliffs, rising in some cases to a thousand feet in height. The formation is extremely friable, and by the action of the elements, enormous masses are continually disappearing beneath the waves of the sea that beat upon this unprotected shore. These tufas differ considerably in consistency at the eastern end of the island. The species is a fine light-red dust that is blown about by the wind and is destitute of vegetation; towards the southwest end the basis is a compact mud-like red clay, while the colossal crowns, intended to adorn the gigantic statues, are carved out of a variety that has been scorified in one of the craters, and is of a dull reddish color.

The ordinary rules for estimating the age of rocks by compactness can be applied at Easter Island only hypothetically, because the scoriform and more dense specimens are found immediately contiguous to one another. In places they are quite conglomerated, as though older formations had been disturbed by volcanic convulsions, while a new flow of lava enveloped and sealed the whole into a heterogeneous mass. During our short stay on the islands there was no opportunity to measure the lava flow or to make investigations of that nature.

Natural caves are numerous, both on the coast-line and in the interior of the island. Some of them are of undoubted antiquity and bear evidence of having been used by the early inhabitants as dwellings and as burial places. It is reported that small images, inscribed tablets, and other objects of interest have been hidden away in such caves and finally lost through land-slides.

The numerous hills on this island have gently sloping sides, except where they approach the coast, falling at this point precipitously to the sea. The plains are irregularly shaped, and some of the smaller ones rise to a considerable height. The physical character of the soil is alluvial. The substratum is volcanic ash and stones, and the upper formation is composed of decayed vegetable matter mingled with a rich deposit of decomposed lava washed down from hills by the frequent rains. These plains being formed by the periodical eruptions of the volcanoes, some difference may be noted in the quantity of the soil, varying according to location.

After the successive discharges of lava from the craters of Rana Roraka and Rana-kao had prescribed the limits of the island and when this flow had ceased, there was a heavy deposit of mud, covering deeply both hill and dale. This condensed earth, after the lapse of centuries, has formed a soil that produces a natural grass affording an excellent pasturage for flocks and herds. The expiring energy of the volcanic power appears to have been directed, long after the formation of this soil, to sprinkling thickly the entire surface of the island with stones and small bowlders, thus providing the means of attraction and holding the moisture, nature's substitute, as it were, for trees. The natives have distinct names for the following varieties: Black and red tufa with volcanic cinder and pumice are called "Maea-Haue-haue," "maea" being the generic term applied to all stone. A soft gray tufa is ground down with the juice of the sugar-cane and used as a paint. This is known as "Kiri-kiri Teu." Hard slates, black, red, and gray, are used for stone axes and called "Maea-Toke." Granite used for the same purpose is known as "Maea-Nerhive. The hardest and finest stone implements are made of the flinty beach pebble known as "Maea-Reng-rengo." The hard cellular stones from which the majority of the platforms are built are called "Maea-Pupura." The material from which images were constructed is called "Maea-Matariki," and the obsidian from which spear-heads were made is known as "Maea-Mataa."

VARIOUS NAMES OF THE ISLAND.

Previous to the general recognition of the name bestowed by Admiral Roggeveen in commemoration of the day upon which the land was discovered, it had not been regularly christened by either of the earlier navigators who claimed to have sighted it. The Spaniards afterwards gave it the name of San Carlos, but the Dutchman's title of Easter Island was preferred by the chart-makers and was adopted by the world in general.

The island is known to the natives as "Te Pito te Henua," the literal interpretation of the words signifying the "navel and uterus." This singular name was given to the land, according to the ancient traditions, by Hotu Metua immediately after its discovery, and has been handed down through succeeding generations unchanged. To the simple-minded Polynesian this name is suggestive, appropriate, and beautiful. The child of nature recognizing the volcanic origin of the island can see in the great volcano, Raua Roraka, a resemblance to the human "te pito" in relation to its shape and gently sloping sides surrounding the shallow crater. The same association of ideas would picture the majestic volcano, Rana Kao, at the southwest end, as "te henua," in whose womb was conceived the embryo and whose vitals brought forth the rocks and earth from which the island was formed.

"Kiti te ciranga" is stated by an English writer of some note to be the native name for the island, but we could not find any authority for it, nor did the natives with whom we came in contact recognize the name.

TE PITO TE HENUA, OR EASTER ISLAND. 453

Throughout southeastern Polynesia this island is known as Rapa Nui, but the name is of accidental origin and only traces back about twenty years. When the islanders, kidnaped by the Peruvians, were being returned to their homes, there was for a time a question as to the identity of those from Easter Island. The native name of "Te Pito te Henua" was not recognized by the French officials, and finding certain fellow-sufferers hailing from Oparo, an island lying 2,000 miles to the westward, were more successful under the local appellation of Rapa iti Little Rapa), the euphonious title was dropped and Rapa nui (Great) Rapa) substituted. Teapy, Waihu, and various other names have been given to the island, but clearly without warrant. Vaihu was the name of a district and was occupied by the most powerful clan in the days of Cook and La Pérouse, but it was never applied to the entire island.

CLIMATE.

The climate is not unlike that of Madeira, with one wet and one dry season. From April to October the rainfall is copious, and in summer it is limited to passing showers. The mean temperature at the time of our visit (midsummer), in the shade, at 2 o'clock p. m., was between 78° and 80° Fah., and at 2 o'clock a. m. there was a fall of about 6 degrees. The southeast trades blow fresh at the beginning and end of the season, and make the climate salubrious and healthful. Our long fatiguing marches, while making the exploration of the island, were not accompanied with inconvenience from exposure to the direct rays of the sun, the constant breezes making the sensible temperature always appear lower than that recorded by the thermometer. Violent exercise induced profuse perspiration, but evaporation was always free and rapid. Electric storms are unknown.

VILLAGES AND HABITATIONS.

The Catholic missionaries built at Vaihu, on the south coast, near Cape Koe Koe, a commodious and substantial church, a parsonage containing three rooms, and several outbuildings. The house is now the residence of Mr. Salmon, the outbuildings are occupied by his employés, and the church has degenerated into a storehouse for wool. The principal native settlement is at Mataveri, on the southwest coast, and about a mile distant, at Hanga Roa, a small neat church has been erected. Here the islanders assemble on Sundays and other occasions to hear the service read by one of their number, who was ordained especially to take charge of this congregation upon the departure of the French missionaries. At the southwest end of the island, and near the base of Rana Kas, is the residence of Mr. Brander.

The house is of modern structure, with large and convenient rooms, but is in a state of bad repair, and is more attractive when viewed from a distance, surrounded by the shrubbery and vines that have been planted about it, than it is upon close inspection.

The native priest and a few of his connections reside at Hanga Roa, only those in the employ of Mr. Salmon live at Vaihu, and the only settlement on the island that may be termed a village is the one at Mataveri. The primitive huts formerly used by the natives (Fig. 1) have

FIG. 1.
NATIVE HOUSES BUILT OF BULRUSHES.

been abandoned for more comfortable dwellings constructed under the direction of a Danish carpenter out of material obtained from the wreckage of several vessels loaded with Oregon lumber. These buildings are of a style of architecture commonly met with in small cheap barns and stables, but to the simple-minded islanders they supply all the comforts that could be desired.

These houses are usually about 25 feet long and 15 feet wide with undressed weather-boards and roofed with the same material. Hinged doors open in the center and admit light and ventilation, though a few of the more pretentious buildings are furnished with small glazed windows. The floors are of bare earth strewn with a litter of dried grass, filthy and vermin-infested from long use. Mats made of bulrushes are spread out for sleeping; several rough bedsteads and chests were seen, but the majority of the houses are destitute of furniture or ornament. Several families occupy the same dwelling; men, women, and children lie down together like dogs in a kennel, and with about the same ideas of what constitutes the comforts of life.

FLORA.

The native traditions agree in the statement that the discoverers of the island found it destitute of trees and all vegetation except grasses and a creeping vine bearing a dehiscent fruit to which the name Moki-oo-ne was given. Hotu-Matua and his followers are believed to have brought with them potatoes, yams, bananas, sugar-cane, and the seed of various plants, including the paper-mulberry and toromiro trees. The newly discovered species of legume, together with fish and turtle, enabled the first settlers to exist while the first crop was being planted and cultivated.

Nothing could be more contradictory than the description which the different voyagers have given of Easter Island. Roggeveen states that it was destitute of trees, but the land was found to be exceptionally fertile, producing bananas, potatoes, and sugar-cane of extraordinary thickness, and concludes by saying that the island, by virtue of its productive soil and salubrious climate, could be made an earthly paradise by careful cultivation. Behrens speaks of trees on the island, but to his romantic eyes the clusters of banana and paper-mulberries were magnified into forests. Captain Cook expresses great disappointment in the expectation that he had formed of this island as a place of refreshment. The only articles of importance obtained were potatoes and yams, and these were only sufficient to serve for a few meals; while the fowls, bananas, and sugar-cane were in such inconsiderable quantities that they were deemed hardly worth mentioning. George Foster writes:

> The island is so very barren that the whole number of plants growing upon it does not exceed twenty species, of which the far greater part is cultivated, though the space which the platforms occupy is inconsiderable compared with what lies waste. The soil is altogether stony and parched by the sun, and the water is so scarce that the inhabitants drink it out of wells which have a strong admixture of brine, and some of our people really saw them drink of the sea water when they were thirsty.

Mr. Foster devoted considerable attention to the investigation of indigenous plants, and his report embraces all of the most important varieties. He found the paper-mulberry carefully cultivated for the purpose of making cloth. The stems were from 2 to 4 feet high, and they were planted in rows among the rocks where the rains had washed a little soil together. The *Thespesia populnea* Carr. (*Hibiscus populneus* Linn.), was cultivated in the same manner, and likewise a *Mimosa*, which is referred to as the only shrub that affords the natives sticks for their clubs and pattoo-pattoos, and wood sufficient to patch up a canoe. Wild celery and a few other small plants were identified as the same species as that which he had found growing in abundance on the shores of New Zealand. He also discovered a variety of night-shade, which the Tahitians use as a vulnerary remedy (*Solanum nigrum*), and speculates as to whether it was used here for the same purpose.

La Pérouse, impressed with a desire to relieve to some extent the destitute condition in which he found the islanders and of contributing essentially and lastingly to their welfare, had ground prepared in which he sowed various kinds of pulse. Peaches, plums, and cherries were planted, also pips of oranges and lemons. The natives were instructed as fully as possible in the care and attention the new plants would require, and made to understand the value of this addition to their resources. Not a trace can be found of the things planted by this generous Frenchman, but whether they were suffered to die out through the ignorance or indolence of the natives may never be known.

We found the lapse of a century had made but little improvement in the resources of the islanders. Trees have been planted around the house of Mr. Brander, at the southwest end of the island, but, with the exception of the fig, acacia, and paper-mulberry, they do not appear to thrive. At various places throughout this land we found small clumps of *Edwardsia*, *Broussonetia*, and *Hibiscus*, but all were dead, having been stripped of their bark by the flocks of sheep, which roam at will over the island. None of these trees were over 10 feet high, and the largest trunk we found would measure about 5 inches in diameter.

The natives are not altogether ignorant of husbandry, though they practice it spasmodically and at a great expense of time and labor, differing in no respect from the customs of their forefathers hundreds of years ago. In the cultivation of yams, potatoes, and taro, the young plants are protected from the fierce heat of the sun by a mulching of dried grass gathered from the uncultivated ground. Bananas are grown in holes a foot or more deep and with sloping sides, designed to catch and hold the rain-water as long as possible about the roots of the plant. Sugar cane is grown in protected spots, and attains the height of about 10 feet. During our peregrinations this succulent plant was extensively used in lieu of something to drink, and proved exceedingly valuable in preventing a parched condition of the throat. The natives have no knowledge of the art of extracting the juice of the cane for the purpose of making sugar.

The sweet potatoes are large and remarkably good. The natives eat them both raw and cooked. Experiments have been made recently with imported white potatoes, but they have been tried in various situations and at different seasons without success. After the first growth they appear like new potatoes, and when planted again they are invariably soft and sweet, and are much less palatable than the indigenous variety. We saw tobacco plants growing in secluded spots, but were unable to determine by whom or when they were introduced. The natives maintain that the seed was included among that which was brought to the island by the first settlers. Tomato plants were also found growing wild, and on several occasions proved a valuable addition to our limited fare.

A wild gourd is common, and constituted the only water-jar and domestic utensil known to the natives. Suitable clay abounds, but the potter's art seems never to have been known on the island. There are two varieties of indigenous hemp.

We saw no flowering plants that are indigenous to the soil. Vervain,

Verbena officinalis, and a few others grow in great profusion, but they grew from cuttings obtained from a French vessel of war.

Ferns of many varieties are common, and grow in profusion in the craters of the volcanoes. Except in a few exposed places, the slopes of the hills and the valleys are covered with a perennial grass. It strongly resembles the Jamaica grass (*Paspalum*) and grows in bunches or tufts, which in the dry season become so slippery as to make the walking both difficult and dangerous. This natural growth supplies ample pasturage for the numerous cattle and sheep owned by Messrs. Salmon and Brander.

To avoid the depredations of the sheep that wander over the island without restraint, the natives are compelled to protect their cultivated patches by stone walls. The volcanic stones furnish the only available material for these barriers, and are thrown loosely together to a height of 5 or 6 feet, and inclose gardens from a few feet square to several acres. The deeply rooted prejudice existing in the native mind against physical exertion that might be avoided, has developed a happy expedient to save labor and at the same time to escape the ravages of the animals lately imported by the foreign residents. Ruins of houses, cairns, platforms, and tombs are thickly scattered over the island; many of the standing walls are sufficiently well preserved and others require but little repair. Within these ancient foundation walls are raised their limited crops of fruit and vegetables; the only disadvantage being the contracted area available for each plot.

MAMMALS.

There are no quadrupeds peculiar to the island except several varieties of rodents. The ancient traditions claim that a goat-like animal was found here by the first colonists, with wide-spreading horns and giving six young at a birth. It is difficult to imagine the foundation for this fancy. We found no representation of such an animal either in the mural paintings or outlined on the sculptured rocks, and diligent search of the débris of the caves failed to disclose any of the bones or traces of mammals.

La Pérouse found the islanders without domestic animals, and left with them two ewes, a she-goat, and a sow, with the male of each species. Their native names indicate the recent addition to the language.

In the caves and among the ruins we saw many rats of great size. The examination of the tombs disclosed the fact that the bones had been frequently gnawed by these rodents, and their nests were sometimes found inside the crania.

There are on the island a few cats as wild as though they had never seen the face of man, though they are descended from feline pets landed by some passing vessel. They have grown to an immense size, and upon several occasions when encountered in the dark recesses of a cave or tomb presented a formidable appearance. Messrs. Salmon & Brander have a herd of 600 cattle, and a flock of sheep numbering 18,000. The cattle are from Chilian stock, are small, averaging only about 400 pounds, and possess no dairy qualities; the cows giving barely enough milk to rear their calves. The sheep were also imported from Chili. The wool is coarse and scant, the average being only about 2 pounds per animal. The export of last year in wool was 16 tons, and was shiped to Europe *via* Tahiti. An effort will be made next year to improve the breed of sheep by introducing blooded rams from Australia. A few tough little horses have been introduced from the island breed of Tahiti, but it is doubtful whether this will ever become an important industry.

BIRDS.

Small birds are altogether absent and, except the ordinary domestic fowl, we found only the tropic or man-of-war bird, petrels, gulls, and a variety of aquatic birds. George Foster observed noddies so tame as to settle on the shoulders of the natives, but he did not conclude that they kept a regular breed of them. The common domestic fowl was found on the island by the early navigators, and it is claimed that they were brought there by the first colonists. They are of the same kind as the common chickens reared at home; their bodies are small, and the legs long, but this is no doubt the result of long in-breeding. The natives all have tame fowls about their dwellings, but there are others in a wild state. We shot some of the wild fowls and found them tough and inferior in taste to those that were domesticated.

FISHES.

Fish has always been the principal means of support for the islanders, and the natives are exceedingly expert in the various methods of capturing them. The bonito, albicore, ray, dolphin, and porpoise are the off-shore fish most highly esteemed, but the swordfish and shark are also eaten. Rock-fish are caught in abundance and are remarkably sweet and good. Small fish of many varieties are caught along the shore, and the flying-fish are common. Eels of immense size are caught in the cavities and crevices of the rock-bound coast. Fresh-water fish are reported to exist in the lakes inside of the craters, but we did not see any of them.

Turtles are plentiful and are highly esteemed; at certain seasons a watch for them is constantly maintained on the sand beach. The turtle occupies a prominent place in the traditions, and it is frequently represented in the hieroglyphics and also appears on the sculptured rocks. A species of crayfish classified by Dr. Philippi, of Chili, as "paparchalu," is abundant. These are caught by the natives by diving into the pools among the rocks, and form an important article of food.

Shell-fish are plentiful. Remains of several varities of univalves were found in the stone houses at Orongo, and frequently met with in the débris of the caves throughout the island.

REPTILES AND INSECTS.

Small lizards are frequently seen among the rocks; the natives claim that a large variety is not uncommon, but we saw nothing of it. No snakes exist, but there are centipedes whose bite is said to be extremely painful, though not attended with serious consequences. Several varieties of butterflies were observed. Myriads of flies infest every part of the island. Vliegen Island was the name given to Riroa, in the Pamotu group, or Low Archipelago, by Schouten in 1616, but we were tormented here by hundreds where we saw tens on the Attol. From the earliest dawn of day to the close of the short twilight, hordes of flies annoyed us; it made no difference whether we skirted the cliffs to windward, climbed the breeze-swept hills, or burrowed in the musty caves and tombs, swarms of flies met us, prepared to dispute every foot of the ground. Whatever may have been the parent stock of the Polynesians, we came to the unanimous conclusion that we had discoverd here the lineal descendants of the flies that composed the Egyptian plague, and can testify that they have not degenerated in the lapse of time.

Fleas occasioned us more annoyance than the flies, because this industrious little insect was untiring in its attentions by day and night. They were found in numbers in all the camping places, and we seemed to get a fresh supply every time a halt was called.

There are fifteen or twenty mangy dogs of a mongrel breed on the island whose hides were literally alive with jumping insects. They had long ago given up all hope of relief, and made no ineffectual efforts in that direction, but they plainly expressed in their mute way the conviction that life in this flea-bitten state was not worth the living.

It was said that there were no mosquitoes on the island until cisterns were built by Messrs. Salmon and Brander to catch the rain-water. We saw none elsewhere.

Cockroaches about 2 inches long, with antennæ to correspond, infest every dwelling on the island, from the humble thatched hut to the comparatively comfortable residences of the foreigners. They partook of our food at meal-times with a freedom which showed that the presence of the stranger caused no restraint; while at night they made themselves familiar with our garments in whatever time could be spared from their gastronomic researches.

A peculiar variety of snapping beetle made its appearance every evening just before sundown, appearing suddenly and vanishing with daylight.

NETS AND ROPES.

Various forms of fishing nets were manufactured, from the hand net to the long seine called "kupenga maito," which was supported by poles at the extremities, weighted with stone sinkers on the submerged edge and floated by billets of wood on the surface (Plate XIII). Their light casting-nets were used with great dexterity as they waded along the beach, and when a shoal of small fish appeared, the net was thrown with the right hand. These nets were remarkably made, and in the manufacture a netting-needle of bone or wood was used, much after the fashion in more civilized countries. The coarse nets and cordage was made from the twisted bark of the *hibiscus*, and the fine ones from the fiber of the indigenous hemp. From the strong heavy ropes used in raising and transporting the colossal images to the light but durable fish-lines, the threads were all twisted by hand, across the knee, into even strands, which were multiplied according to the size and strength required.

NATIVES.

The population of Easter Island is not stated in actual figures by any of the traditions or legends, but all agree in the statement that the different districts were peopled by numerous and powerful clans who were constantly at war with each other. The immense amount of work performed by the image-makers and platform-builders would indicate the employment of a great many persons, if accomplished within a reasonable limit of time, or the extension over several centuries, if the undertaking was carried out by successive generations. The ruins of extensive settlements near Tahai Bay Kotatake plains, around Puka Manga-Manga mountain, the Rana-Hana-Kana coast, the vicinity of Anakena, the shores of La Pérouse Bay, and extending along the coast from Tongariki to Vinapu in an almost unbroken line, would prove either the presence of numerous inhabitants, or a frequent change of location. The limited area of the 32 square miles of surface available for cultivation precludes the idea of any very dense population, and many reasons might be assigned for a frequent change of habitation. We know that the stone houses at Orango were only occupied during the feast of "bird eggs." The image-builders engaged in the quarries of Rana Roraka probably lived at Tongariki, and entire communities may have changed location at different seasons of the year from failure of water supply, or some equally sufficient reason.

The early Spanish voyagers estimated the population at between 2,000 and 3,000. Admiral Roggeveen states that he was surrounded by several thousand natives before he opened fire upon them. Captain Cook, fifty-two years later, placed the number at between 600 and 700, and Foster, who was with him, estimated them at 900. Twelve years later (1786) La Pérouse placed the population at 2,000. Bushey (1825) puts the number at about 1,500. Kotzebue and Lisiansky make more liberal estimates. Equally chimerical and irreconcilable deductions are made by recent writers. Mr. A. A. Salmon, after many years' residence on the island, estimates the population between 1850 and 1860 at nearly 20,000. The diminution of the actual number of inhabitants progressed rapidly from 1863, when the majority of the able-bodied men were kidnaped by the Peruvians, and carried away to work in the guano deposits of the Chincha Islands, and plantations in Peru. Only

FISH-NET.

(Cat. No. 129746, U. S. N. M. Easter Island. Collected by Paymaster W. J. Thomson, U. S. N.)

NATIVES OF EASTER ISLAND.

a few of these unfortunates were released, and all but two of them died upon the return voyage, from small-pox. The disease was introduced on the shore and nearly decimated the island in a short time. An old man called Pakomeo is at present the only survivor of those returned from slavery, and he is eloquent in the description of the barbarous treatment received from the hands of the Peruvians. In 1864 a Jesuit mission was established on the island, and through the teachings of Frère Eugene, the ancient customs and mode of life were replaced by habits of more civilized practice.

H. M. S. *Topaze* visited the island in 1868. At that time the population was about 900, one-third of the number being females. In 1875 about 500 persons were removed to Tahiti under contract to work in the sugar plantations of that island. In 1878 the mission station was abandoned, and about 300 people followed the missionaries to the Gambier Archipelago.

Mr. Salmon took a complete census of the people just before the arrival of the *Mohican*, and we were furnished with a list containing the names of every man, woman, and child on the island. The total number of natives is at present 155. Of these 68 are men, 43 women, 17 boys under fifteen years of age, and 27 girls of corresponding age. The population has been for several years at a standstill, the births and deaths being about equal in numbers. The longevity of the islanders appears to compare favorably with the natives of more favored lands. The oldest man among them is a chief called Mati; his actual age is not known, but he must be upwards of ninety, and his wife is nearly of the same age.

The last king was kidnaped by the Peruvians and died in captivity, but his nearest descendant is a sturdy old fellow (Fig. 2) called Kaitae,

FIG. 2.
KAITAE, NEAREST DESCENDANT OF THE LAST KING OF EASTER ISLAND.

about eighty years of age. The simple mode of life, frugal diet, freedom from care and anxiety, with regular habits, are favorable to the longevity of the race.

PERSONAL APPEARANCE OF THE NATIVES.

In describing the personal appearance of the islanders (Plate XIV) the early writers give us a pleasing variety to choose from. Behrens solemnly states that a boat came off to the ship steered by a single man, a giant 12 feet high, etc. He afterwards observes, "with truth, I might say that these savages are all of more than gigantic size. The men are tall and broad in proportion, averaging 12 feet in height. Surprising as it may appear, the tallest men on board of our ship could pass between the legs of these children of Goliath without bending the head. The women can not compare (Fig. 3) in stature with the men, as they are

FIG. 3.
NATIVE WOMEN.

commonly not above 10 feet high." Roggeveen does not commit himself to a measurement, but states "the people are well proportioned of limb, having large and strong muscles, and are great in stature. They have snow-white teeth, which are uncommonly strong; indeed, even among the aged and gray we were surprised to see them crack large hard nuts whose shells were thicker than those of our peach seeds." La Pérouse contradicts the account as to their enormous height and praises the beauty of the women, who, he says, resemble Europeans in color and features. M. Rollin states that the females were more liberally endowed with grace and beauty than any which were afterwards

GROUP OF NATIVES IN EMPLOY OF MR. BRANDER.

met with. The natives are not of large stature; a few of the men are tall, but they are of spare build, stand erect with straight carriage, and appear taller than they really are.

Great care was taken to measure accurately the human remains found in the oldest tombs excavated on the island. These proved the ancient islanders to have been of medium size, and the largest skeleton found measured a little short of 6 feet. The men are strong, active, and capable of standing great fatigue—a fact demonstrated to our satisfaction during the exploration of the island. The women are shorter and of smaller bone than the men, as is usually the case throughout Polynesia.

Mendana states that the islanders are nearly white and have red hair. They resemble the Marquesans more than any other Polynesians, and considerable variety prevails in their complexions. The children are not much darker than Europeans, but the skin assumes a brown hue as they grow up and are exposed to the sun and trade-winds. The parts of the body that are covered retain the light color, and the females, who are usually protected from the sun, are much fairer than the men. Bronze complexions are believed to indicate strength, and a dark skin is considered a mark of beauty. The eyes are dark-brown, bright, and full, with black brows and lashes not very heavy. The countenance is usually open, modest, and pleasing. The facial angle is slightly receding, the nose aquiline and well proportioned; the prominent chin with thin lips gives somewhat the appearance of resolution to the countenance.

The native character and disposition has naturally improved as compared with the accounts given by the early navigators. They were then savages wearing no clothes, but with bodies painted in bright colors. The women are said to have been the most bold and licentious in Polynesia, if the reports are correctly stated, but we found them modest and retiring and of higher moral character than any of the islanders. The repulsive habit of piercing the lobe of the ear and distending the hole until it could contain bone or wooden ornaments of great size is no longer practiced, but there are still on the island persons with ear-lobes so long that they hang pendent upon the shoulders. In disposition the natives are cheerful and contented. Our guides were continually joking with each other, and we saw no quarreling or fighting. They are said to be brave and fearless of danger, but revengeful and savage when aroused. They are fond of dress and ornaments. Very little tappa cloth is now worn, the people being pretty well equipped with more comfortable garments, obtained from the vessels that have called at the island. (Plate XV). Straw hats are neatly braided by the women and worn by both sexes. The women wear the hair in long plaits down the back, the men cut the hair short and never discolor it with lime as is the custom in many of the islands of Polynesia. The hair is coarse, black, and straight, sometimes wavy, but never in the kinky stage. The beard is thin and sparse. Gray hair is common among those beyond middle life and baldness is very rare.

Kava is not grown upon the island and the drink made from the kava-root, common throughout the South Sea, is not known to these people. The diminution of the inhabitants can not be ascribed to the introduction of intoxicating drinks, or indeed any of the factors usually advanced in such cases. The decadence was no doubt accelerated by the introduction of the small-pox, and by the deportation of large numbers, but it is earnestly hoped that the small remnant of the people will increase and multiply under the comforts and protection acquired from contact with civilization.

BRUTAL TREATMENT OF NATIVES BY EARLY VOYAGERS.

The brutal treatment that the islanders received from the hands of their early visitors was not calculated to impress them favorably. Usually the strangers were met upon their arrival by a crowd of noisy, restless, impetuous people, as curious as children and as peaceable and friendly with all their boisterousness. The greatest fault they committed was theft, and in return numbers were shot down and innocent persons murdered. Roggeveen plainly states that his boats approached the island well armed and in great fear of the natives. The men were formed in line of battle as they disembarked, and before all were landed, some one in the rear fired a shot, and immediately a fusilade began by these cowardly ruffians upon the unfortunate islanders, ten or twelve of whom were killed outright and as many were wounded. The admiral quietly shifts the responsibility for this outrage upon the shoulders of the second mate of the *Thienhoven*, who offers as an excuse that some of the natives were observed to take up stones and make threatening gestures. As soon as the astonishment and terror of the inhabitants had subsided, they sued for mercy, and everything they possessed in the way of fruits and vegetables, poultry, etc., was procured and laid as a peace offering at the feet of the Dutchman. Captain Cook afterwards received the most friendly reception possible from the same people, but he observed their great dread of fire-arms, the deadly effects of which were thoroughly understood. The landing party conducted a brisk trade, and were highly amused to witness the small thefts committed upon one another in order to obtain articles for barter, yet Lieutenant Edgecomb did not hesitate to immediately shoot with his musket a poor unfortunate who picked up a little bag of botanical specimens.

Captain Beechey was received with friendly demonstrations and his boats, sent on shore for supplies, obtained bananas, yams, potatoes, sugar-cane, nets, etc., in trade, and some were thrown into the boats, leaving the strangers to make what return they chose. His journal dwells at great length upon the thieving propensity of the natives. His boats were surrounded by native swimmers, who made off with small articles that came within reach of them, and among them were women who were not the actual plunderers, but who procured the opportunity for others by engrossing the attention of the seamen.

To reach the landing-place the boats had to pass a small isolated rock upon which many persons had congregated, and who sang a song of welcome, accompanied by gestures showing that the visit was acceptable. On shore the party was surrounded by a crowd clamorous to obtain something from the strangers, the few presents offered were accepted, and then everything that came handy appropriated in the most open manner. This led to a scuffle, in which sticks and stones were freely used, resulting in a fight in which the native chief was shot and killed. The punishment of the natives, according to European ideas, was both cruel, and unnecessary. La Pérouse judged the same crimes more leniently, and did not feel justified in committing murder to avenge petty thefts. The outrages perpetrated upon the defenseless people by Captain Rugg, of the *Friend*, and other freebooters, including the Peruvian slavers, require no comment.

THIEVING.

The natives did not attach any moral delinquency to the practice of thieving. They had a god of thieving, and successful operations were believed to be accomplished under his patronage, and only detected when not sanctioned by that spirit. The detected thief was made to suffer for his crime by an established system of retaliation peculiar to themselves, but the individual never lost caste or the respect of his friends. Thieves caught in the act might be beaten, knocked about, and the aggressor was permitted to offer no resistance in the efforts to escape, although he might be the largest and most powerful. Before the retaliation could be enforced, the theft had to be proven and fixed beyond question, then the plundered individual was at liberty to recover the value of the loss from any property available belonging to the robber, and in the event of the value not being recovered, articles of value could be destroyed to equalize the amount. Retaliation for theft could be enforced by the weak and feeble against the strong and powerful, and any resistance would call to their aid the entire community.

The rite of circumcision, so common throughout Polynesia, is unknown here, and their language contains no equivalent word for it. At the present time, all the natives have professed Christianity, and the ancient customs have been replaced by the ceremonies of the church to a great extent, but since the departure of the missionaries there has been a tendency to return to the old ideas, and many superstitious and practices are mingled with their religion. The marriage ceremony is performed by the acting priest in the church, but the practice is permitted with children who have not reached the age of puberty, and the betrothal is conducted by parents, the relations of the female paying a stipulated amount, generally in food to be consumed by the friends at the feast given to celebrate the event. It is not certain that polygamy ever existed, but an ancient custom permitted the husband to sell or lease his wife to another for a stated term. On account of the disproportion in the number of the sexes, celibacy was a matter of necessity, and probably originated this custom. Love of family is a strong trait in their character; children are fondly cared for, and the desire for offspring is general.

TATTOOING.

Tattooing is not practiced at the present time, none being observed upon children and young persons. But all those advanced in life are ornamented on all parts of the body. Unlike the Samoans and other islanders, where a standard pattern is adhered to, the designs were only limited by the fancy and ability of the artist. Both sexes were tattooed (Figs. 4, *a* and *b*), but the women to a greater extent and with more elaborate designs than the men. The material used in tattooing is obtained by burning the leaf of an indigenous plant called "ti," which is moistened with the juice of a berry called "poporo." A tattoo comb is made of bone or fish bones fastened to a stick, which is held in position and struck with a sharp blow.

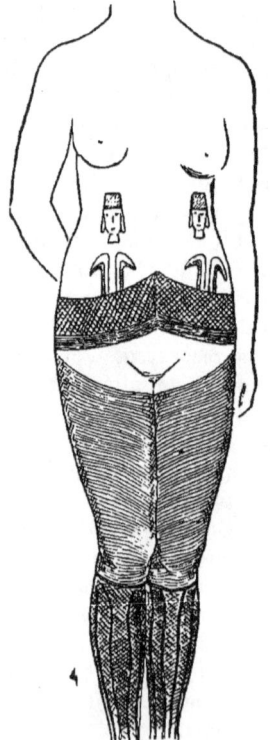
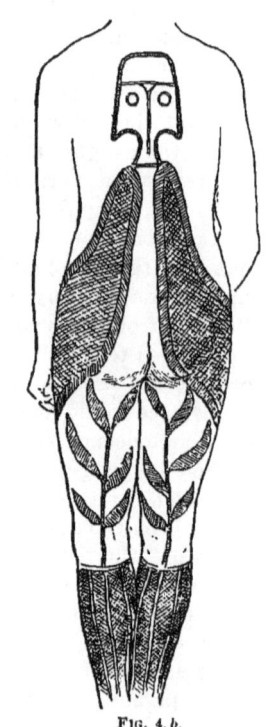

FIG. 4, *a*.
TATTOOING ON NATIVE WOMAN (FRONT VIEW).

FIG. 4, *b*.
TATTOOING ON NATIVE WOMAN (BACK VIEW).

The highest ornamentation was as follows: A narrow band around the upper part of the forehead, at the edge of the roots of hair, with little circles extending down upon the forehead and joined to the band by a stem. From the coronet, a line extended around the outside edge of the ear, with a circle on the lobe. The lips were freely tattooed, after the manner of the Maoris, with lines curving around the chin and extending towards the cheek-bones; the entire neck and throat covered with oblique or wavy lines, with occasional patches of solid coloring; a broad, wide girdle (Fig. 4, a) about the waist, from which bands rise in front and behind, representing trees and foliage, surmounted by large faces on the breast and back, and smaller ones on each side of the body. Below the waist belt the lines were fine, like lace-work, and from the thigh to the knee the appearance was that of silk tights with variegated pattern. Below the knee there were various designs. terminating in a point at the feet.

SALUTATION.

The form of salutation is "Kohomai," literally interpreted, "Come to me." This is always heartily expressed, and parties meeting often shout out the kohomai while some distance apart. The greeting is varied by the addition of a word of respect when addressed to a superior in rank, or a stranger, and by a term of endearment, when to a child or to a relation.

DRESS.

The costume of the natives is at present made up of the cast-off clothing obtained from ships of all nations that have called at the island, but principally old uniforms of the French, Spanish, and English vessels of war. Brass buttons appeal strongly to the native love for adornment, and many were made happy by the liberal contributions from the *Mohican.* Very little tappa cloth is made on the island at present, but specimens of the ancient handiwork are treasured up in every family. The mode of manufacture is quite similar to that practiced on the various groups of the South Sea, but the patterns are much less elaborate. The bark is stripped from the branches of the *Hibiscus,* in a manner to obtain the greatest possible length, and rolled into coils with the inner bark outside, in order to make it flat and smooth. It is then scraped with a piece of obsidian to remove the bark, the coils being occasionally soaked in water to remove the resinous substances. The strips are laid across a log and beaten for many hours with a heavy mallet. The mallets are made of the heaviest and hardest wood that can be obtained (*toromiro*), about a foot long and 3 inches on each face, some of which are smooth and others carved into grooves or ribs, to suit the different stages in the process of manufacture. Several strips of bark are beaten into one thickness of cloth, according to the purpose for which it was intended, some being made quite fine and others coarse and heavy. No gum is used except that naturally contained in the bark, and the fibers adhere closely when kept dry. The fabrication of the tappa speaks well for the native invention and industry, but it is not very durable when compared with woven goods. The colors with which the decorations are made are procured from roots, leaves, and berries of indigenous plants and are prepared with considerable skill. Several kinds of earth are used for the dark colors, the pigment being ground down and boiled in the juice of the sugar-cane.

MATS.

The natives excel in the manufacture of fine mats, specimens of which will be found in our collection. They are made of bulrushes obtained from the craters in the vicinity of the lakes formed by the collection of the rain-water. They are woven by hand, and fine specimens are highly prized.

AMUSEMENTS.

The amusements of the people were reduced to a minimum when the customs of their heathen forefathers were abandoned, and at present there is no general assemblage for the purpose of enjoyment except an occasional marriage feast or some accidental occasion, such as the arrival of a foreign ship. Prominent among the ancient customs were feasts to celebrate the return of the different seasons and various anniversaries in their history, such as the landing of Hotu-Metua at Anakena Bay. Upon the latter occasion the ancient traditions were repeated by recognized orators, and a prominent feature of all fetes was athletic sports, such as running, spear-throwing, and feats of skill and dexterity. Dancing was the most common of all amusements and there was no assemblage without its appropriate dance.

THE NATIVE DANCE.

Just as the traditions are cherished and repeated from father to son, the native dances are remembered and held in esteem, although never publicly practiced. Mr. Salmon secured the services of the "star performers" and we were fortunately enabled to witness the peculiarities of the native dance at his house at Viahu, on the eve of our departure from the island. The music was furnished by three persons seated upon the floor, who accompanied their discordant voices by thumps upon a tom-tom improvised from old cracker-boxes, and the dance was performed by an old woman and a young girl, the latter possessing some claim to symmetry of figure. The dancers wore a single loose garment, short enough to expose the bare ankles and sun-browned feet. Over the head and shoulders was thrown a white cloak, composed of a few yards of cotton cloth, which was sometimes spread open and occasionally made to hide the whole figure as they went through the various evolutions of the dance. This mantle was not managed with any particular skill or grace and seemed to be identified with one particular dance, after which it was discarded for the small dancing-paddle or wand. The weird songs related the achievements and exploits of their ancestors in war, fishing, and love, and the gestures of the dancers were upon this occasion perfectly proper and modest. Some of the movements were suggestive of a rude relationship to the dances performed by the geisha girls of Japan in their odori, and consisted of movements and attitudes calculated to display the elegance and grace of the performers. The peculiar feature of the native dancing is the absence of violent motion; there is no jumping or elaborate pirouettes, no extravagant contortions, and nothing that might be called a precision of step. The lower limbs play a part of secondary importance to the arms and the dancers indulge in no dizzy gyrations. The feet and hands are kept moving in unison with the slow, monotonous music, while the dancers endeavor to act out the words of the song by pantomime. These islanders, like their sisters throughout Polynesia, have their hula-hula, or dances that partake of passion and abandon, and portray the old story of coquetry, jealousy, and ultimate surrender of the maiden. Soft swaying movements, a gentle turning away, timid glances, and startled gestures, gradually giving place to more rapturous passion, speak plainly enough the theme of the song, though the movements are less graceful and elegant than those which characterize the nautch dances of India. Among the diversified dances, some are performed by men and others by women, but the sexes rarely if ever dance together. Wands are usually held in each hand, but occasionally one and sometimes both are discarded. Feather hats and other ornaments are worn in portraying characters and some of the dances are said to be of obscene tendencies.

RELIGION.

Like most savage nations, the Easter Islanders had numerous superstitions and resorted to charms, prayers, incantations, and amulets to bring good luck and ward off evil. A thorough delineation of these superstitions might be instructive in the light of showing the real depth of the religious feeling of those who now profess Christianity as well as the capacity of the native mind for entertaining a higher form of civilization; but, unfortunately, our brief stay on the island did not afford time to thoroughly investigate the subject.

The belief in a future state was a prominent feature in the religion. After death the soul was supposed to depart to the "place of departed spirits" to be rewarded by the gods or tormented by the demons. With this idea in view a small hole was invariably built in the wall near the top of all tombs, cairns, and other receptacles for the dead, by which the spirit of the deceased was supposed to find egress. Deified spirits were believed to be constantly wandering about the earth and to have more or less influence over the human affairs. Spirits were supposed to appear to sleeping persons and to communicate with them through visions or dreams.

Gnomes, ghouls, and goblins were believed to inhabit inaccessible caves and niches in the rock and to have the power of prowling about after dark. The small wooden and stone images known as "household gods," were made to represent certain spirits and belong to a different order from the gods, though accredited with many of the same attributes. They occupied a prominent place in every dwelling and were regarded as the medium through which communications might be made with the spirits, but were never worshiped. The Great Spirit Meke-Meke is represented by a bird-like animal as referred to in the description of sculptured rocks and paintings at Orongo.

SUPERSTITIONS.

The islanders were superstitious to an extent that was extraordinary, and they were constantly under the influence of dread from demons or supernatural beings. Fish-hooks were made of bones of deceased fishermen, which were thought to exert a mysterious influence over the denizens of the deep. Fishermen were always provided with the stone god that was supposed to be emblematic of the spirit having cognizance of the fish. Rocks in certain localities were believed to be under spirit taboo, and persons who walked over them were punished with sore feet. The leaves of several harmless plants were regarded as prophylactic against disease. Stones were buried beneath the doorways of houses to guard against evil influences. The native priests were simply wizards and sorcerers who professed to have influence with evil spirits sufficient to secure by incantations their co-operation in the destruction of an enemy, or by occult means gain their aid and good-will for the protection of property, crops, etc. The system of taboo corresponds with the same thing practiced throughout the islands of the South Sea, and included a prohibition in regard to persons as well as property. The symbol of the taboo on crops properly consisted of a small pile of stone placed in the form of a pyramid, or piled one on top of the other. The natives have a way of divining the future by means of a flower, common enough in more civilized countries but not observed before in Polynesia. "Ae" and "Aita" are repeated as the petals are thrown away, and the signification appears to be equivalent to the "yes," and "no" of Goethe's Marguerite.

SACRIFICIAL STONES.

In the rear of some of the best-preserved platforms are stones said to have been erected for sacrificial purposes. These altars consist of a single shaft, generally of vesicular lava, but in some cases cut from the material of which the images and crowns were made. They range in height from 5 to 10 feet, squared to $3\frac{1}{2}$ or 4 feet on each face, and stand in the center of a terrace paved with smooth bowlders. The sides and plinth were covered with figures sculptured in low relief, but are now too much weather-worn to be traced. These altars are said to have been designed and used for human sacrifices, but of this a reasonable doubt may be expressed. The form is inconveniently adapted to the purpose and the stones differ in all respects from those used for the same purpose in the other islands. Evidences of fire on top of stones were plain enough, but no charred bones were found except those of recent date belonging to sheep and cattle.

DISEASES AND THEIR TREATMENT.

The practice of relieving pain by manipulation of the body was the effective movement cure resorted to by the islanders years before the Swedish or massage treatment assumed its present prominence. Without entering upon the question of how valuable the practice of lomi-lomi may be as a cure for ailments, I may testify to the physical regeneration of this titillant manipulation. On more that one occasion I have thrown myself upon the ground, completely exhausted by over-exertion, and yielded to the dexterous kneadings and frictions and palmings and pinchings of those skilled in the treatment. The hard-fisted native is by no means gentle in the operation, but with palms and knuckles vigorously tests every muscle and tendon, as well as every joint of the vertebræ, until the exhausted patient sinks into a state of oblivious somnolence.

Several of the plants indigenous to the island were considered valuable remedies for certain ailments, but the chief therapeutic art of the native practitioner was the pretended exercise of powers of divination. The application of herbs, simples, and the practice of lomi-lomi were perhaps not sufficient distinction, and therefore a claim was made for occult knowledge and supernatural power.

The native pharmcopœia is extremely limited in its scope. The thistle is bruised and applied to sores and ulcers, arrowroot for burns, and a species of nightshade is used as a vulnerary remedy. On this breeze-swept island diseases of a paludal nature are unknown.

A mild type of remittent fever is common during the rainy season from April to October, but nature is left to fight its battles without assistance. Rheumatism and pulmonary complaints occasionaly result from long exposure to inclement weather, but as a rule no medical treatment is attempted.

The natives believe that a disease called "kino," or cracked feet, results from walking over the rocks along the shore at Tabai. Probably the trouble arises from cuts and abrasions coming in contact with a succulent vine that grows at this place.

FIRE.

The method of obtaining fire requires considerable preparation of material and patience on the part of the operator. A pointed stick of hard wood is rubbed against a piece of dry paper-mulberry until a groove is formed, which finally becomes hot from the friction and ignites the lint or fiber thrown up at the end of the groove. This is blown into a flame, and dried grass added to it until the fire is sufficiently established. The difficulty of preserving suitable material in a perfectly dry state led to the custom of keeping up a perpetual fire in each community. These vestal fires were kept up by persons appointed for that purpose, though it does not appear that they were vestal virgins. Caves affording ample protection from the weather were selected for the location of these permanent fires, and although they had no religious significance, the flames were as carefully watched and attended as the celestial fire of the followers of Zoroaster.

CANNIBALISM.

The traditions abound with instances of anthropophagism, and in all Polynesia there were no more confirmed cannibals than these islanders. The practice is said to have originated with a band of natives who were defeated in war and besieged in their stronghold until reduced to the borders of starvation. From this time the loathsome custom of devouring prisoners, captured in war, grew in popular favor. Cannibalism may have originated in a spirit of revenge, but it grew beyond those limits, and not only were prisoners of war and enemies slain in battle eaten, but every unfortunate against whom trivial charges were made met that fate. Instances are related in the legends of children being devoured by their parents, not from any other motive than to satisfy the cravings of their depraved and vitiated appetites. Cannibalism was practiced until a comparatively recent period. Several of the older natives acknowledge that they had frequently eaten human flesh in their youth, and described the process of cooking and preparing "long-pig" for the feast.

GOVERNMENT.

The ancient government of Easter Island was an arbitrary monarchy. The supreme authority was vested in a king and was hereditary in his family. The person of the king was held sacred. Clan fights and internecine struggles were common, but the royal person and family were unmolested. The king reigned over the entire island and was not disturbed by the defeat or the victory of any of the clans. The island was divided into districts having distinct names and governed by chiefs, all of whom acknowledged the supremacy of the king. The title of chief was also hereditary, and descended from father to son, but the king reserved the right to remove or put to death any of them and of naming a successor from the people of the clan.

There was no confederation, each clan being independent of all the rest, except as the powerful are naturally dominant over the weak. The chiefs wore peculiar feather hats to denote their rank, and they presided at feasts and councils in the absence of the king. Other grades of rank were recognized, such as that required by feats of valor, public service rendered, such as image making, etc., but this privileged class had no authority vested in them over their fellows. Personal security and the rights of private property were little regarded, and disputes were settled by king or chief without regard to law or justice. There was no code of laws, the people avenged their own injuries, and persons who incurred the displeasure of the ruler were marked as victims for sacrifice. It does not appear that any great homage was paid the king, and no tax was exacted of the people. Long-continued custom was accepted as law, and defined the few duties and privileges of the private citizen.

Maurata, the last of a long line of kings, together with all of the principal chiefs of the islands was kidnapped by the Peruvians and died in slavery. Since that time there has been no recognized authority among the natives; every man is his own master, and looks out for his own interests.

In 1863–'64 the natives were converted to Christianity by Frère Eugène, a Jesuit missionary. A Frenchman called Dutrou-Bornier had settled upon the island and started an extensive farm, and a conflict of authority sprang up between the two foreigners, which led to bitter feuds between the natives. Dutrou-Bornier lived with a common woman, who had been the wife of a chief, and he succeeded in having her proclaimed queen of the island, under the name of Korato. A system of espionage and intrigue was instituted by Queen Korato, guided by the Frenchman's instructions, which resulted in an open rebellion against the ecclesiastical authority. The missionary was finally compelled to leave the island, and he removed to Gambier Archipelago with about three hundred of his followers, giving Dutrou-Bornier and Queen Korato a clear field. The Frenchman was killed in August, 1876, by being thrown from his horse while drunk, and Queen Korato and her two children survived him only a few years. Mr. Salmon found upon his arrival that none of the natives had assumed authority over his fellows, and in due course that gentleman became to all intents and purposes the king of the island, ruling the people with kindness and wisdom and thus securing their unbounded respect and esteem.

BURIAL OF THE DEAD.

Hundreds of tombs, cairns, platforms, and catacombs were examined during our stay on the island, and in all cases the bodies were lying at full length. In a vault beneath platform No. 11 are a number of skulls packed together in sufficient quantity to completely fill the compartment—trophies of war perhaps, in view of the fact that the skulls were those of adults; but in no single instance did we discover the remains doubled up as the Incas and other American aborigines were in the habit of burying their dead. In the early ages it was the custom to wrap the corpse in dried grass, bound together by a mat made of sedge, and whether laid in platform, cairn, or cave, the body was usually laid with the head towards the sea. Succeeding generations substituted tappa or native cloth for the sedge mat, and the present people are sufficiently civilized to prefer rude coffins when the material can be obtained. Cemeteries were located by the missionaries near the churches at Vaihu and Mateveri, and strong efforts made to discourage the burial of converted natives with their heathen ancestors, but they were never able to overcome their aversion to promiscuous interment.

BOATS.

Hotu-Matua is said to have landed upon the island with three hundred followers in two canoes, which are described in the traditions as 90 feet in length and 6 feet deep (draught of water). From the description given of these boats and the representations found of them among the mural paintings and sculptures in certain caves, the canoes of the original settlers were quite similar to the Fiji war-canoes. They were constructed of many pieces of wood neatly fitted together and held in place by thongs or lashings; high and sharp at both ends and balanced by an outrigger or smaller canoe. Such boats are in use at the present time in many of the Polynesian islands and are quite capable of making long voyages at sea. The boats built by succeeding generations were few in number and small in size, on account of the scarcity of material to be found on the island. Many of the early navigators refer to the scarcity of boats belonging to the natives. Captain Cook saw several canoes, 10 or 12 feet long, built of pieces 4 or 5 inches wide, and not more than 2 or 3 feet long, but the majority of his native visitors swam off to his ship. Captain Beechey saw three canoes on the beach, but they were not launched. Von Kotzebue saw three canoes each containing two men. At the time of our visit the only boats on the island were two large ones, belonging to Messrs. Salmon and Brander, built of material obtained from the wrecks on the coast. There are no canoes in use at the present time, but we found two very old ones in a cave on the west coast, having long ago passed their days of usefulness on the water and now serving as burial-cases. They were a patchwork of several kinds of wood sewed together, and though in an advanced stage of dry-rot the material was sufficiently well preserved to prove that it never grew on Easter Island, but had been obtained from the drift-wood on the beach.

WEAPONS AND WAR.

The native weapons in offensive and defensive operations were limited to obsidian-pointed spears, short clubs, and the throwing-stones, but these were handled with remarkable skill and dexterity. The history of the simple weapons in the hands of people who became preeminent in their use has been repeated in all ages and countries, and is fully exemplified in these islanders; though their primitive spear, lacking the metal-piercing medium, could never aspire to the fame of the gladiator's trident, the Homeric javelin, the Roman pilum, the Turkish jereed, the Landsknecht's halberd, the Polish lance, the Zulu assagai, or even the knobkerry of the Amazulu. The formidable weapon of the ancient Parthian, still wielded by the dexterous Turcoman, was not known to these islanders. Arrows might have been improvised, but there was no wood in their possession suitable for the manufacture of bows.

Unlike the Fijians and other Polynesians to the westward, who did great execution with their long war clubs, these natives used in fighting only the patoopatoo, or the meré, like that of the Maori, except that they were invariably made of wood. They possessed a long club, a little expanded and flattened at one end, and the other carved into a head with a double face with eyes made of obsidian and bone; but this was carried as a batôn of office before the chiefs and used only for that purpose.

Stones were thrown with great precision and accuracy from the hand, and the use of a sling, such as made David more than a match for the gigantic Philistine, appears to have been unknown. Slings were common among the Incas and other races of South America from the earliest times, but no traces of such an appliance could be found on Easter Island, either in the tombs or mentioned by the ancient traditions.

A want of practice has probably made the natives of to-day less proficient in stone-throwing than their forefathers, but if the stories may be believed, the time was when their truculent address could only have been surpassed by Runjeet Singh's Akalis in flinging the chuckkra.

Several of the ancient traditions speak of a net being used in fighting, and men were especially trained in its use, but whether they resembled the old Roman *retiarius* can not be discovered, the custom having long since died out. It is unknown to the natives of to-day.

Two kinds of spears were used, one about 6 feet long for throwing and the other a shorter one; a heavier stabbing pike was only fit for use at close quarters. In its original form the spear was essentially a missile, and the traditions speak of the adoption of the thrusting weapon in the desperate engagements that resulted in the extermination of the "long-eared race." The shafts were made of *pourou Hibiscus* sp. and *tu Dracœna terminalis*, and the various forms of obsidian points were secured by a lashing made from the indigenous hemp. The javelins were thrown underhanded with the little finger foremost, but they did not have that peculiar vibratory motion that distinguished the Zulu assagai.

Nothing was known of a retrieving weapon, such as the boomerang of the Australians, or even the throwing-sticks of the Eskimo tribes on the coast of Alaska.

There was no class of professional fighters or soldiers; every able-bodied man was supposed to be a warrior and compelled to do duty in time of war. Fighting men were not trained or drilled, except that throwing stones and darting the spear were favorite amusements and always a prominent feature of all feasts. The clans were always led to battle by the chief, but there was no particular formation. Every man acted in accordance with his individual fancy, or as occasion demanded, relying upon skill and strength alone. No shields were used and no particular efforts were made to parry the weapons of the enemy.

In view of the fact that the islanders all acknowledged the authority of one king, their wars were surprisingly numerous, barbarous, and unrelenting. The traditions are filled with accounts of sanguinary conflicts originating from trivial causes and continued through generations, until one party or the other were entirely exterminated. The slaughter on the field of battle was never very great, but in the event of a general defeat, the vanquished party was pursued by the victors to their hiding places, their habitations destroyed, females captured, children and infirm persons brutally murdered. The defenseless unfortunates who fell victims to their merciless captors, accepted their fate, whether it was slavery, torture, or butchery, with remarkable fortitude, seldom if ever making any show of resistance.

EXPLORATION OF THE ISLAND.

The *Mohican* came to anchor in the roadstead of Hanga Roa (Plate XVI) on the morning of Saturday, December 18, 1886. The individuals most interested in the exploration of the island went on shore without delay, and the work was pushed forward as rigorously as possible until the hour appointed for the sailing of the ship for Valparaiso on the evening of the last day of the year.

Messrs. Salmon and Brander boarded the ship upon her arrival and extended the hospitalities of Easter Island, placing their limited resources entirely at our command with a heartiness that won our immediate esteem, and which ripened into sincere friendship before our departure. These gentlemen are closely connected with the royal family of Tahiti, and we had been intrusted with letters and various articles from relatives and friends who desired to embrace the opportunity for communication offered by the *Mohican*.

Upon landing at Hanga Roa we found nearly all of the natives on the island congregated to receive their unknown visitors. The men inspected us closely and were profuse in friendly demonstrations, while their wives and daughters gazed curiously from a little distance, and the children's manner plainly showed the enjoyment of an occasion of infrequent occurrence in their quiet lives. Surrounded by this crowd we walked about a mile to the house of Mr. Brander, where the baggage, tools, and impedimenta in general were deposited. During the afternoon a reconnaissance was made to the crater of Rana Kao and the ancient stone-houses in the vicinity, and in the evening we crossed the island in a light wagon with Mr. Salmon to his residence at Vaihu. That gentleman has, during his long residence on the island, accumu-

Report of National Museum, 1889.—Thomson.

CRATER OF RANA KAO.

ANCIENT STONE-HOUSES AT ORONGO, FROM WHICH PICTURED SLABS WERE PROCURED.

lated a valuable collection of curios and relics of the former inhabitants. Nearly all of our first night on shore was devoted to the purchase and cataloguing of specimens from Mr. Salmon's collection, all of which will be referred to and described elsewhere. Duplicates were obtained of all articles furnished Lieut. Commander Geisler, of the *Hyane*, for the museum at Berlin, and of those collected by the *Topaze* for the British Museum, together with original tablets and other relics of great interest and value that had escaped the attention of former collectors.

RECONNAISANCE TO RANA KAO.

Sunday, December 19.—Made an early start from Vaihu and rode to the central elevations called Mount Teraai, Mount Punapau, and Mount Tuatapu and inspected the quarries from whence the red tufa was obtained which formed the crowns or head-dresses that ornamented all the huge images. Following the road to the southwest we made the ascent of Rana Kao. The crater is nearly circular and about a mile in diameter (Plate XVII), with steep jagged sides, or walls, except on the south, where the lava-flow escaped to the sea. A lake fills the bottom of what was once the volcanic caldron; the water is of great depth and the surface covered with a coat of peat, so dense and strong that cattle range over it, finding food at irregular intervals. The surface of the lake is about 700 feet from the top, but the cattle have made a path by which the descent can be made with safety.

Skirting the edge of the crater to the southward the ridge becomes narrower, falling precipitously a thousand feet to the sea on one side, and descending abruptly into the crater on the other until it terminates in an elongated wall of rock rising to a sharp, jagged edge impassable to either man or beast. Just where this elevated edge contracts rapidly towards the south are located the ancient stone-houses of Orongo. (Plate XVIII). These burrow-like dwellings were built with little regard to streets, avenues, etc., but were regulated by the contour of the land. Piles of débris in one or two spots marked the destroying hand of former investigators, but the large majority of the houses were intact, and in some instances the openings had been sealed up with stone, making it difficult to outline the original entrances. These dwellings were constructed without windows or other openings except a door-way so low and narrow that an entrance could only be effected by crawling upon the hands and knees, while in many cases it was necessary to creep serpent-like through the contracted confines. Many interiors were inspected by the light of candles provided for the purpose and houses marked for thorough investigation on the morrow.

While tracing and sketching the sculptured rocks in the vicinity of Orongo, the declining sun hastened the departure for Vaihu, where the hours after our evening meal were devoted to making notes of the native traditions as translated by Mr. Salmon, until that good-natured gentleman could be kept awake no longer. It had been proposed that we should occupy one of the ancient stone houses for the night, in order to be near the scene of operations planned for the next day, but they were damp and ill-smelling and the work accomplished on the traditions more than repaid the time lost in recrossing the island.

THE ANCIENT STONE HOUSE AT ORONGO.

December 20.—Leaving Vaihu at early daylight we arrived at Hanga Roa in time to meet the detachment of eight selected men sent on shore from the ship with proper tools and implements for making a thorough exploration of Orongo and vicinity. (Plate XIX). The blue-jackets scampered up the slope of Rana Kao with the buoyant spirits of school-boys out for a holiday, and arriving at the spot were anxious to lend the assistance of willing hands and plenty of brawn to the prosecution of the work.

Every house was entered and inspected, though occasionally a miscalculation was made in the dimensions of a narrow passage-way and it became necessary to rescue a prisoner by dragging him back by the heels. Once inside the building, the interior could be easily inspected and sketches made of frescoes and sculptured figures. (Plate XX).

These remarkable habitations were built against a terrace of earth or rock, which in some cases formed the back wall of the dwelling (Fig. 5). From this starting point a wall was constructed of small slabs of stratified basaltic rock, piled together without cement and of a thickness varying from about 3 feet to a massive rampart of 7 feet in width.

FIG. 5.
VIEW OF STONE HUT IN ORONGO.

The outer entrance is formed by short stone posts planted in the ground and crossed by a basaltic slab. The passage-way was in all cases unpaved and usually lined on the top and both sides with flat stones. This important feature added materially to our comfort while forcing an entrance through some of the narrow openings, and saved the necessity for adding to our already bountiful supply of bruises and abrasions. No regularity of plan is shown in the construction of the majority of the houses; some are parallelogram in shape, others elliptical, and many are immethodical, showing a total absence of design, the builder being guided by the conformation of the ground, the amount of material available, and other chance circumstances. These houses

Removing Slabs from House at Orongo.

Ancient House at Orongo

are roofed with slabs of rock of sufficient length to span the side walls, showing that no particular care had been exercised to form close joints. Over this stone ceiling the earth was piled in mound-shape, reaching a depth in the center of from 4 to 6 feet, and covered by a sod that afforded ample protection from rain. The floors were the bare earth, and the interiors were damp and moldy from insufficient ventilation afforded by the single contracted opening.

An accurate measurement of these remarkable structures gave the average height from floor to ceiling 4 feet 6 inches; thickness of walls, 4 feet to 10 inches; width of rooms, 4 feet 6 inches; length of rooms, 12 feet 9 inches; average size of door-ways, height 20 inches, width 19 inches. In making the survey of Orongo the houses were

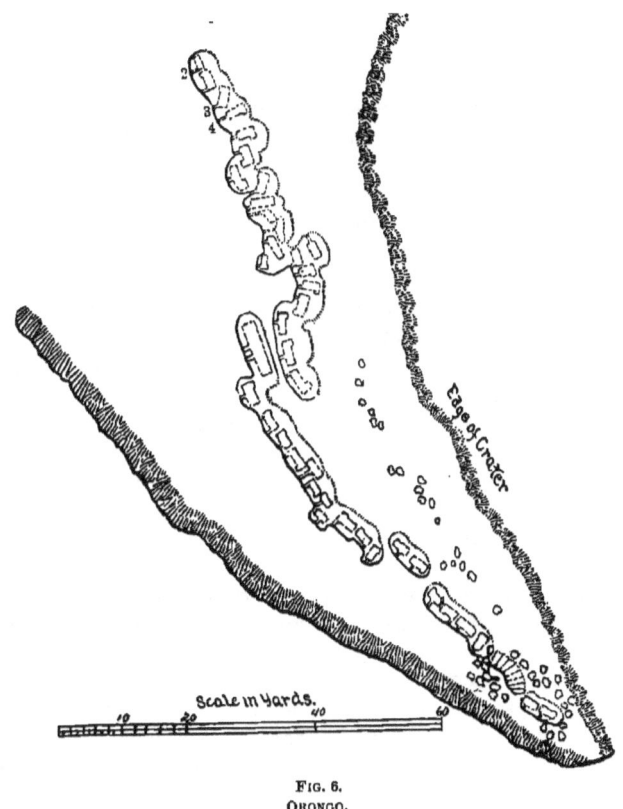

FIG. 6.
ORONGO.

numbered from 1 to 49, inclusive, commencing at the inshore extremity (Fig. 6). While in the majority of instances the interior dimensions were considerably below the average given above, several of the houses exceeded those limits, particularly in the length of the rooms. The largest house contained a single chamber nearly 40 feet long; three were over 30 feet, and eight measured over 20 feet in length, with other dimensions approximately the same as the general average. These rude dwellings were not in all cases confined to a single apartment; some have one and a few have two or three recess chambers opening out of the main room; but they were dark little dens, having no separate light or ventilation.

Near the center of this assemblage of houses there is a sort of square court with eight door-ways opening upon it. These might be considered separate and distinct dwellings, though the apartments are connected by interior passage-ways, making it possible to pass from one to the other. At the extreme end of the point a similar collection of houses opens upon a circular court, and the interiors are also connected.

In front of each house and about 10 feet from the door-way, small excavations lined with slabs of stone, making holes about a foot wide and 2 feet long and about 20 inches deep, indicated the culinary arrangements of the former inhabitants. The *modus operandi* of preparing the food was primitive in the extreme; a fire was built in the rude oven and removed when the stones were sufficiently heated, a covering of damp earth being placed over the oven to retard the radiation of heat.

Thorough examination demonstrated the fact that these peculiar houses were not precisely alike in all respects, though the same general characteristics prevailed. Those at the extreme point of the ridge (Plate XXI) bear evidence of great antiquity, and much excavation was necessary before a satisfactory examination could be made of the doorposts or stone supports to the entrances, which were covered with hieroglyphics and rudely carved figures. From houses numbered 2, 3, and 4 (Fig. 6) on Lieutenant Symond's chart of Orongo, were taken samples of these sculptures for the National Museum. The large beach pebbles were obtained by digging to a depth of 2 feet below the door-posts, and are of considerable interest both from the dense nature of the material and the fact that these carvings were found frequently repeated throughout the island.

The majority of the houses at Orongo are in a fair state of preservation and bear evidence of having been occupied at no very remote period. The result of the investigation here showed very little of carving on stone, but the smooth slabs lining the walls and ceilings were ornamented with mythological figures and rude designs painted in white, red, and black pigments. Houses marked 1, 5, and 6 on Lieutenant Symond's chart were demolished at the expense of great labor and the frescoed slabs obtained. Digging beneath the door-posts and under the floors produced nothing beyond a few stone implements.

The houses in this vicinity occupy such a prominent position that they were naturally robbed of everything in the way of relics by the natives, who were beginning to appreciate the value of such things through the importance placed upon them by the foreign vessels that

GROUP OF VERY ANCIENT HOUSES AT THE EXTREME END OF RIDGE AT ORONGO, SHOWING SCULPTURED DOOR-POSTS.

SCULPTURED ROCKS AT ORONGO.

have called at the island. A niche in the wall of each of these dwellings was evidently designed to receive the household god and the various valuables which were possessed by the inhabitants. Whatever treasures they may have held in former years, we found them empty, and our search revealed nothing of importance.

Attention was directed to one of the buildings in this assemblage that apparently had no entrance way. One wall was demolished, disclosing a rude coffin containing the remains of a native recently deceased. The unoccupied house had been utilized as a tomb, and sealed up with the material of which the walls were built.

SCULPTURED ROCKS.

The most important sculptured rocks on this island (Plate XXII) are in the immediate vicinity of the stone houses at Orongo (Fig. 7). As

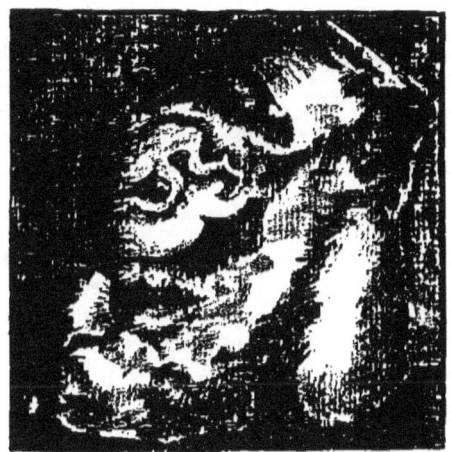

FIG. 7.
SCULPTURED ROCKS NEAR ORONGO.

much time as possible was devoted to examining and sketching these curious relics. The hard volcanic rock is covered by carvings intended to represent human faces, birds, fishes, and mythical animals, all very much defaced by the ravages of time and the elements (Plate XXIII). The apparent age of some of the rock-carvings antedates the neighboring stone houses, the images, and other relics of the island except the ruined village on the bluff west of Kotatake Mountain. Fishes and turtles appear frequently among these sculptures, but the most common figure is a mythical animal, half human in form, with bowed back and long claw-like legs and arms. According to the natives, this symbol was intended to represent the god "Meke-Meke," the great spirit of the sea (Fig. 8). The general outline of this figure rudely carved upon the

FIG. 8.
SCULPTURED FIGURES OFTEN REPRODUCED ON ROCKS AT ORONGO: "MEKE-MEKE."

rocks, bore a striking resemblance to the decoration on a piece of pottery which I once dug up in Peru, while making excavations among the graves of the Incas. The form is nearly identical, but, except in this instance, no similarity was discovered between the relics of Easter Island and the coast of South America.

ANCIENT CUSTOMS IN RELATION TO GATHERING THE SEA-BIRDS EGGS.

From the most reliable information that could be obtained, the stone houses at Orongo were built for the accommodation of the natives while celebrating the festival of the "sea-birds eggs," from a remote period until the advent of the most important ceremonies.

During the winter months, sea-birds in great numbers visit the Island to lay their eggs and to bring forth their young. The nests are made among the ledges and cliffs of the inaccessible rocks, but a favorite spot for these birds has always been the tiny islands Mutu RauKau and Mutu Nui, lying a few hundred yards from the southwest point of the island (Plate XXIV). Here the first eggs of the season are laid, and therefore Orongo was selected as a convenient point to watch for the coming of the birds. According to the ancient custom, the fortunate individual who obtained possession of the first egg and returned with it unbroken to the expectant crowd, became entitled to certain privileges and rights during the following year. No especial authority was

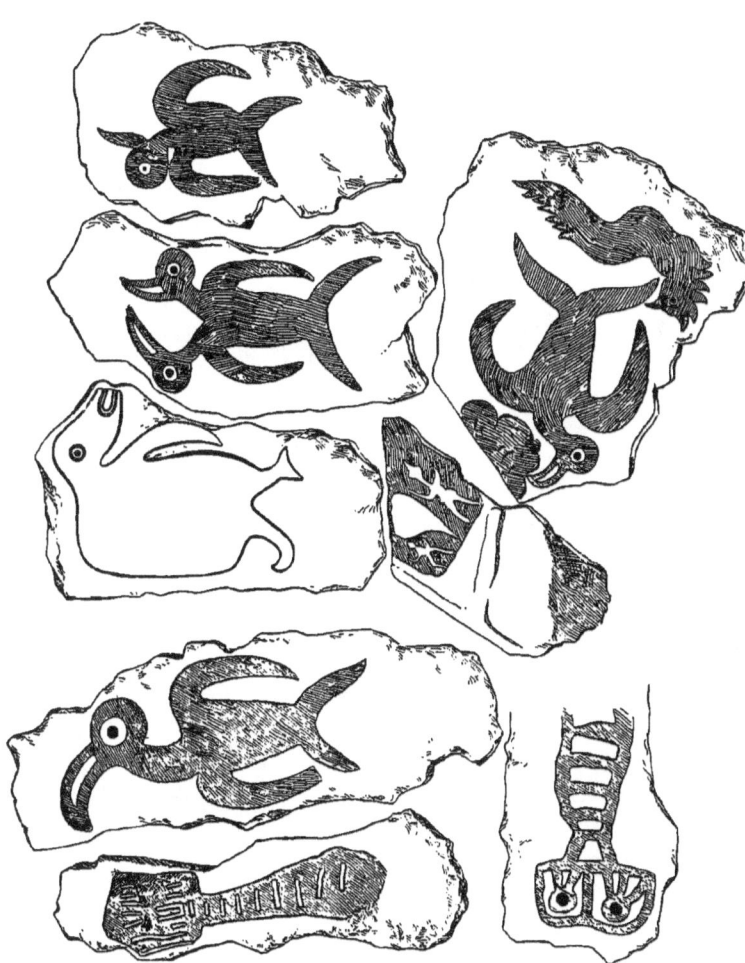

PICTURED SLABS TAKEN FROM THE ANCIENT STONE-HOUSES AT ORONGO.
(Cat. No. 128373-128376, U. S. N. M. Easter Island. Collected by Commander B. F. Day, U. S. N.)

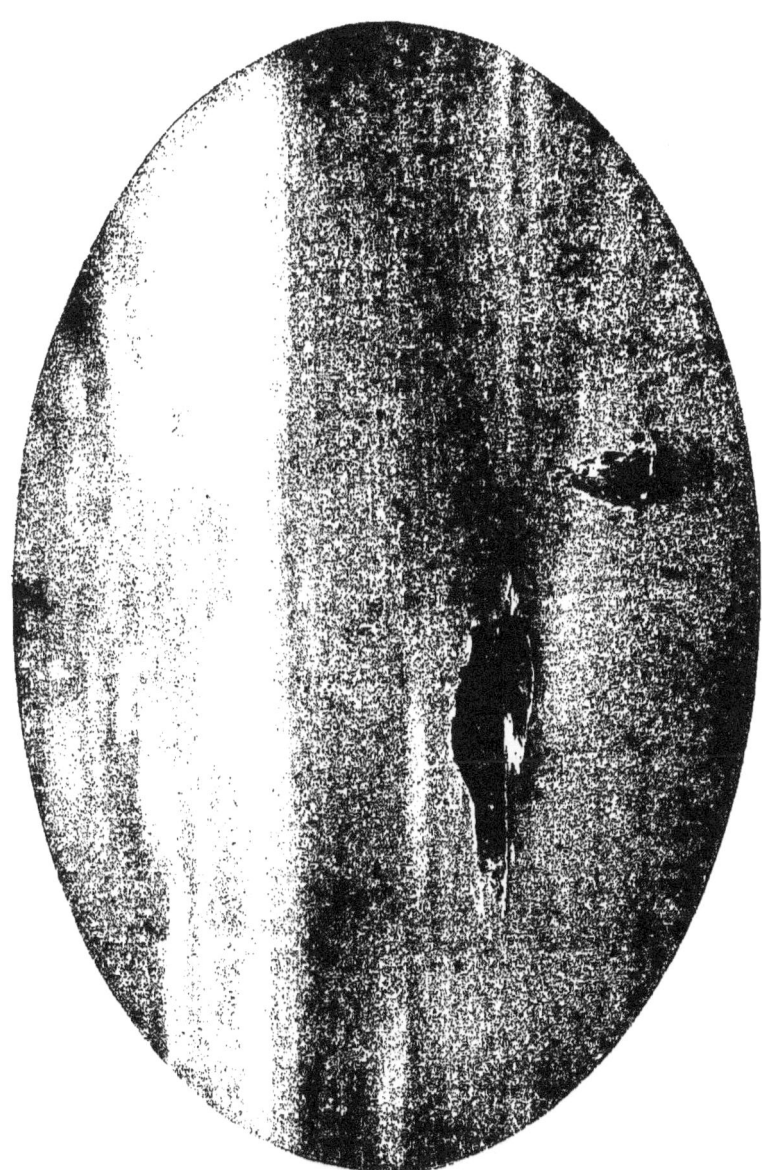

Mutu Raukau and Mutu Nui; Islands near Rapa Nui, where Birds' Eggs were gathered.

vested in him, but it was supposed that he had won the approval of the great spirit "Meke Meke" and was entitled to receive contributions of food and other considerations from his fellows. The race for the distinguished honor of bearing off the first egg was an occasion of intense excitement. The contestants were held in check at Orongo until the auspicious moment arrived, and the scramble commenced at the word "go," pronounced by the king, who was about the only able-bodied man on the island who did not participate. It was decidedly a go-as-you-please race, every man selecting his route to the sea by the circuitous paths or directly over the face of the cliff, and many fatal falls are recorded as the result.

The swim to Mutu Rau Kau was a trifling matter, the chief difficulty being to return with an egg unbroken through the general scramble.

The houses at Orongo were probably unoccupied except for a short period in July of each year while awaiting the coming of the sea-birds. The peculiarity of their construction might be accounted for by the fact that the thatched hut, common to the plains, could not be used to advantage on this exposed bluff. The low, contracted entrances, were used here as well as elsewhere for defense. Factional fights were common, and it was necessary that every house should be guarded against surprise and easily defended. Another reason might be found for making the openings as small as possible, in the absence of doors to shut out the storms. The sculptured rocks in the vicinity of Orongo bear record of the grateful contestants in the egg-races to the great spirit "Meke Meke" for his benign influence and protection, much after the manner in which boats, pictures, and other objects are dedicated to certain patron saints in more civilized portions of the earth.

EMPLOYMENT OF NATIVES.

The investigations in the vicinity of Orongo having been finished, a contract was made with Mr. Brander for removing from the excavations and transporting to the landing-place the frescoed slabs, inscribed doorposts, and objects collected, and the evening was devoted to the native traditions until exhausted nature demanded a few hours rest. With a view of propitiating the natives and securing their good-will and co-operation in prosecuting the work with the utmost dispatch, a number of men were employed to assist in the excavations made at Orongo, but the experiment proved a failure. They constituted themselves an appreciative audience, and could not be induced to work. They evinced a lively interest in all that was going on, and performed astounding gastronomic feats at meal-time. We concluded to dispense with their services after a demonstration of their dexterity in causing the disappearance of every small object that remained unprotected for a moment. Several of the head-men, afterwards employed as guides to accompany the expedition around the island, and stimulated with the hope of bountiful rewards, performed valuable service in the way of locating waterholes, identifying localities, naming objects of interest, etc.

December 21.—Preparations were made for an early start on the expedition already planned. The native contingent was dispatched about daylight with camp equipage and instructions to form Camp Mohican at a spot where it was reported good water could be found in abundance. We were somewhat handicapped for the march by the fatigue of the last few days, added to the want of rest. The hospitality of the Brander establishment had been cordially extended, but such a large and varied assortment of insects and noxious animals had possession of the premises, that we preferred the open air, though there were several passing showers during the night. A working party from the ship, consisting of nine men, including a boatswain's mate and quartermaster, landed at an early hour, each man equipped with knapsack, canteen, shovel and pick. The expedition took the road passing through the villages of Mataveri and Hanga Roa to the coast, followed by almost every man, woman, and child on the island. The interest displayed by the natives in our movements gradually died out after a few hours of hard walking, and towards noon the last party returned to their homes, leaving us a clear field.

Following the coast-line to the northwest, every part of the ground was carefully examined, platforms measured and plotted, excavations made, and objects of interest collected and catalogued.

Near Anahoirangaroa Point, on some ledges of hard volcanic rock we found numerous depressions that evidently were made at the cost of great labor. Some are elliptical in shape, others perfectly circular, averaging about 3 feet in diameter and 2 feet deep. The majority are above high-water line and others just awash when the tide is full. No explanation could be obtained in regard to these holes, and it was concluded that they were originally intended as live-boxes for the preservation of fish.

The natives have a superstition to the effect that any one who walks over these rocks will be afflicted with sore feet, and we received many solemn warnings in regard to it. If there is any foundation for it at all, it is probably due to a succulent vine that grows here, coming in contact with the wounds caused by the sharp rocks. A short distance farther on stands a round tower 12 feet in diameter and 20 feet high (Fig. 9), said to have been erected as a lookout station from whence the movements of turtles could be watched. We found here, as well as under every other pile of stones of any description on the island, tombs and receptacles for the dead, all filled with human remains in various stages of decay, from freshly interred bodies to the bones that crumbled into dust upon exposure to the air. The entire island seems to be one vast necropolis, and the platforms along the sea-coast appear to have been the favorite burial places in all ages. Natural caves were utilized as places of deposit for the dead.

Considerable time was devoted to the examination of the platforms,

TE PITO TE HENUA, OR EASTER ISLAND.   485

and in numerous instances interesting catacombs and tombs were discovered, containing remains of great antiquity. In this connection a peculiar trait in the native character was developed. Towards evening one of the native guides returned to pilot the working party to the place selected for the camp, just at the time a particularly old tomb had been uncovered and the crania were being removed from their former resting place. This the unsophisticated native took in at a glance, and with the announcement that we were desecrating the burial place of his forefathers, he set up a howl of despair, and became prostrated with grief at the sight of a skull which he claimed to recognize as that of his great grandfather. Notwithstanding the absurdity of the statement, the anguish displayed induced us to return the bones to their ancient resting place. The afflicted youth quickly dried his eyes, and intimated that for a suitable reward he would be willing to dispose of the remains of his ancestors, and he thought that a consideration of about $2 would assuage his grief. That settled it. The skulls were gathered into the collection, and the sorrowing native left to mourn the loss both of the money and of the bones of his forefathers.

FIG. 9.
OBSERVATION TOWER ON BLUFF NEAR ANHOIRANGAROA POINT.

Many of the stone bases upon which the images stood still remain in their original positions upon the platforms. Generally they are irregular in shape, a few have been squared, and on platform No. 5 we found one of octagon shape that stood the test of measurement very well. Between platforms 4 and 5 the land falls away gently to the sea, and this slope is paved regularly with small round bowlders, having every appearance of having been constructed as a way for hauling out boats. The coast in this vicinity is perfectly rock-bound, but a narrow channel extends from the paved way out to sea. Boats might land here at any time. With the wind southeast, or in any direction except west, the landing would be perfectly smooth. The place is admirably adapted to the landing of heavy weights, but, as far as known, the images were never transported by sea, nor did the islanders possess boats sufficiently large to float them, or material from which they could be constructed.

CAVE AND TOMB NEAR AHUAKAPU POINT.

On the face of the cliff near the point, Ahuakapu, a large and interesting cave, was visited. Many of the recesses and angles had been walled up and contained human remains. Fossiliferous specimens of marine animals were obtained by digging up the floor of the cave. The igneous rocks in the vicinity show evidences of rude sculptures, among which could be traced canoes, fishes, and men in various attitudes. Upon the extreme point we found another one of those round towers, built for the purpose of observing the movements of turtles on the beach. The shaft measures $24\frac{1}{2}$ feet, and stands in the center of a narrow platform 67 feet long, filled with tombs containing human remains that had long been undisturbed, as evidenced by a luxuriant growth of lichens on the rough rocks.

RUINS OF THE OLDEST HABITATION ON THE ISLAND.

On the high bluff west of Kotatake Mountain we discovered the ruins of a settlement extending more than a mile along the coast-line and inland to the base of the hill. These remains bear unmistakable evidences of being the oldest habitations on the island. The houses are elliptical in shape, with door-ways facing the sea, and were built of uncut stone. Some of the walls are standing, but the majority are scattered about in the utmost confusion. An extremely interesting feature of these ancient ruins is the fact that each dwelling was provided with a small cave or niche at the rear end, built of loose lava stones, which was in a number of instances covered by an arch supported by a fairly shaped key-stone. The recesses were undoubtedly designed to contain the household gods, and the key-stone, although extremely rough in construction, is unmistakable in its application. Our guides had no knowledge of this locality and knew no distinctive name for it.

Messrs. Salmon and Brander had not visited the spot, because the location is bleak and desolate and, as far as they had heard, was a trackless waste, devoid of all interest.

TE PITO TE HENUA, OR EASTER ISLAND.

Camp Mohican was formed a few hundred yards in the rear of platform No. 7. We reached the spot just as the shades of night were closing in, foot-sore and weary from the hard day's march. The camp was not more than 5 miles in a direct line from our starting point in the morning, but we had traveled many times the distance in making a thorough inspection of the ground. A narrow pathway follows the coast-line for a part of the distance, which affords safe footing for the natives; everywhere else the ground is covered with volcanic rocks of every conceivable size and shape, making the walking both difficult and dangerous. The site for the camp was selected because of the proximity of a water-hole, the only one to be found in this neighborhood. It proved to be a shallow cave where the rain-water collected from the drainage of the surrounding hills; the fluid was full of both animal and vegetable matter and decidedly unpleasant to taste and smell. A shelter-tent was improvised by suspending a blanket at the ends from boarding pikes planted in the ground, and after a hasty meal all hands sought the much needed rest. About midnight ominous looking clouds rolled up from the southeast, and it rained in heavy squalls until morning. Wet and unrefreshed, we turned out at daylight to resume the march with everything completely saturated from underclothing to note-books, but with undaunted resolution to continue the work in spite of the elements.

Platforms 7 and 8 are within a few hundred yards of each other and close to the edge of the bluff, which is at this point 390 feet above the sea level. From beneath these ancient piles many interesting specimens of crania were obtained, together with obsidian spear-heads and stone implements. An extensive settlement must have been located here at a comparatively recent period. Narrow curbing stones indicated the position of the houses. These stones had been squared, with 2-inch holes sunk in the upper face at short intervals to receive the ends of the poles that supported the thatched roof. These dwellings had been built upon terraces descending towards the sea, and though they differed greatly in size, the same characteristics were preserved in all cases. The style of architecture must have been suggested by an inverted canoe. The curbing walls of the house in the center of this collection measured 124 feet in length, 12 feet wide in the center, and converging to 15 inches at the ends.

NATURAL CAVES.

Among some outcropping rocks near by, a cave was accidentally discovered, with a mouth so small that an entrance was effected with difficulty. Once inside, however, it branched out into spacious chambers that could shelter thousands of people with comfort. It bore evidences of having been used in former years as a dwelling-place, and probably had other entrances and extensions which we failed to penetrate for the want of time. Human remains were found in this cave, but all very old.

The caves of Easter Island are numerous and extremely interesting in character. They may be divided into two classes: those worn by the action of the waves, and those due to the expansion of gases in the molten lava and other volcanic action. The process of attrition is in constant progress around the entire coast-line, and the weaker portions of the rock are being undermined by the incessant beating of the ocean. Some of these sea-worn caves are of considerable extent, but generally difficult of access and affording little of interest except to the geologist. The caverns produced by volcanic agencies are found throughout this island, and some were traced through subterranean windings to an outlet on the bluffs overlooking the sea. They are generally quite dry; the rain-water falling upon the surface occasionally finds its way between the cracks or joints in the solid rock, but these gloomy passages and chambers lack grandeur from the entire absence of stalactites and deposits of carbonate of lime. No glistening and fantastical forms of stalagmitic decorations exist here to excite the fancy and create in the imagination scenes of fairy-like splendor. The feeble rays of our candles were quickly absorbed by the somber surroundings, heightening the apparent extent and gloom of the recesses. Careful investigation proved that all of the caves visited had been used as dwelling-places by the early inhabitants.

Platform 18 deserved more attention than we were able to give to it, the facing-stones having been torn from their original position in the structure and lying scattered about as though thrown down by some great convulsion of nature. Some of them show evidences of having been ornamented with rude figures carved on the hard rocks; but the approach of sundown hastened our steps toward Motukau Point, where we could see the flags flying over our camp. The day's march had been exceedingly fatiguing on account of the rugged nature of the ground and the absence of water, but the last mile or so was accomplished at a swinging pace in view of the fact that the camp could not be reached after darkness had closed in. 'Our course had been around Cape North, and covering the territory between the coast and the base of Rana Hana Kana.' Loose bowlders of every imaginable shape and size cover the ground, threatening sprained limbs and broken bones at every incautious step, as though the expiring energy of the volcanoes had been expended in creating this natural barrier.

Camp Day, named in honor of our commanding officer, was located in a district known as Vai-mait-tai (good water), but it was decidedly a misnomer, the supply being ample, but brackish and ill-smelling. After a hearty meal of mutton, prepared by our guides in true island style, we sought shelter under the lee of an outcropping rock, fatigued enough to sleep through the attacks of myriads of noxious insects and regardless of the passing showers of rain.

ANAKENA BAY.

December 23.—A dip in the sea at daylight, and a breakfast of mutton which had been slowly roasting all night on hot stones placed in the ground and covered with earth to prevent the escape of heat, put us in prime condition for the work in hand. Our route lay along the north coast of the island and around Anakena Bay, the place where Hotu-Matua and his followers landed when they arrived from the unknown and much-disputed locality from which they migrated. On the sand beach of this bay we found the small univalve, the remains of which were noticed in all the caves and ruins on the island and which are still highly esteemed by the natives as an article of food. Jelly-fish, such as are known to the sailors as "Portuguese men-of-war," also abound, and are esteemed a delicacy by the natives. The entire plain back of Anakena (La Pérouse) Bay is covered with small platforms, cairns, tombs, and the ruins of dwellings of various sorts. Houses built of loose stones, nearly circular in shape, are plentiful; but they belong to a comparatively recent date, as is indicated by the fact that the stones, of which they are constructed, have been taken from the platforms and from the foundations of the thatched tents. Any sort of material that came handy appears to have been freely used by the builders of these houses. In several we found well-cut heads that had formerly ornamented image platforms, built in the walls, some facing inside and others in the opposite direction. The ruins in the vicinity show that this had been the site of a large settlement, and that it continued to be a place of importance through many generations; but the greatest mystery is how such a number of people obtained a sufficient supply of fresh water.

Near Anakena is a large image in the best state of preservation of any found about the platforms of the island. The traditions assert that this was intended to represent a female, and that it was the last image completed and set up in place. Our guides informed us that it was only thrown down about twenty-four years ago, and previous to that time it had remained for many years the only statue standing upon a platform on the island. Camp Whitney was located at Hangaoue Bay, where we found shelter in a bug-infested cave. The water supply was obtained from an ancient tomb near by, and was both scant in quantity and nasty in quality. We were, however, in such an indifferent state of mind that anything wet was acceptable.

December 24.—With the knowledge that we had a particularly hard march before us, we struck camp early and got under way before it was fairly light in the morning. Around Cape Pokokoria the rugged nature of the ground passed over was extremely exhausting. The slopes of Mount Puakalika are in places covered with coarse hummock-grass and flowering vines, which look green and attractive during the rainy season of the year, but which were at this time almost as dry and parched as though scorched by fire. The toilsome march of this day was heightened by the absence of water, and all suffered severely from thirst.

Starting out in the morning with empty canteens, our throats soon became dry and painful. A small quantity of water was found in the afternoon in Mount Puakatika crater, thick and unpleasant to look upon, but affording valuable relief to our sufferings.

THE POIKE PLAINS.

The Poike Plains are extensive tracts of fine red volcanic sand and dust with occasional patches of hummock-grass struggling for existence in this barren waste. Manga Tea-tea (White Mountains), so called from the grayish appearance of the rocks, furnished the stone implements of the natives. The material was chipped as nearly as possible into the desired shape and then ground down to a point or edge by friction upon a hard surface with sand and water. At Anakena and other points convenient to the sand beach we found grinding-stones, together with unfinished and broken implements.

The traditions assert that the island was in former ages densely populated, and the legends are supported by the gigantic works of the image and platform builders and the ruins of various sorts scattered about. While the accounts are probably greatly exaggerated in regard to the number of inhabitants at one time, there is every reason to believe that the people were numerous enough to severely tax for their support the limited area of ground available for cultivation. The Incas of Peru usually selected for burial-places the rocky and steep slopes of the hills or the low sandy plains, where cultivation was impossible, and presuming that a similar economy might have been practiced here, much time was devoted to a thorough examination of the sand-wastes at the eastern extremity of the island. Excavations were made at the expense of great labor in several places where the indications were most promising, but with barren results. Digging to a depth of 9 feet in a depression near Cape Anataavanui we found several flat stones of large size, such as were used for facing the platforms, but the loose, shifting nature of the sand made it impossible with our small force to thoroughly investigate them. The trade-winds freely sweep these elevated plains, blowing the sand about, and creating ridges that may be leveled again by stronger currents at some other season. Hills and depressions simply represent the force and direction of the wind at the time.

TONGARIKI.

Camp Baird was delightfully located in a commodious cave called Ana Havea, on the bay of Hanga Nui, near Point Onetea, and its proximity to Rana Roraka where all the monoliths on the island had been quarried. Tongariki with its rich remains of platforms, images, cairns, and tombs, and Vaihu and other points not yet explored, were sufficient to induce a permanent establishment during the remainder of our stay at Easter Island. The cave was dry, with spacious entrance exposed to the full force of the trade-winds, and we were comfortable to a degree, after dried grass and bulrushes had been collected to sleep upon. Successive generations of natives probably occupied this ancient cavern; an extensive corral has been built near by, and Messrs. Salmon and Brander sleep here while rounding up their cattle. Drinking-water, the great desideratum on the island, obtained from sources that form the crater of Rana Roraka, was, owing to its animal and vegetable impurities, unpalatable, while the supply from the springs was more so, but afforded a pleasing variety, which enabled us to exercise a preference for some other, whenever either kind was used. The so-called springs are holes into which the sea-water percolates, and are as salt as the ocean, at high tide, and decidedly brackish at all other stages.

December 25.—The forenoon was devoted to the exploration of the face of the bluff to the eastward of Tama Point. Many caves were reached after difficult and dangerous climbing, and were found to contain nothing of interest, while others of traditional importance were inaccessible from below, and we were not provided with ropes and the necessary appliances for reaching them from above. No doubt there are caves in this vicinity with contracted entrances that have been covered by loose rocks and intentionally concealed. One such cavern was found by accident. It contained a small image about 3 feet high, carved out of hard gray rock. It was a splendid specimen of the work and could be easily removed to the boat-landing at Tougariki. Retracing our steps toward the camp, the ground between Puakalika elevation and Rana Roraka was thoroughly examined during the afternoon. The plain is completely covered with cairns, tombs, and platforms. Many of the most promising were completely demolished and the foundations dug up to a depth of six feet. All contained human remains in various stages of decay, and the earth upon which they were built proved to be a rich loam filled with sea-shells of minute size, free of stones, while outside of the foundation-walls the composition was composed of bowlders of all sizes with very little earth. Among the vast ruins are many fragments of images and crowns scattered about, and it is evident that platforms were erected and destroyed by succeeding generations. The traditions assert, and appearances indicate, that this plain had from the earliest times been one of the most densely populated districts on the island. Only the remains of walls and cisterns were found here. They were generally small, the largest being 9 feet in diameter, 14 feet deep, and surrounded by a sloping bank paved with small stones to facilitate the collection of rain-water.

In honor of the day, work was suspended earlier than usual, and we returned to camp a couple of hours before sundown, but we found that our Christmas cheer had been reduced to "hard-tack" and island mutton by the leger-de-main of our native assistants, though ample stores had been provided for the entire expedition. With no indulgence in indigestible Christmas luxuries, we were enabled to retire to an undisturbed rest at an earlier hour than would have been probable in a more civilized land and with different surroundings.

December 26.—Our native contingent deserted in a body at daylight on the plea that their religious convictions would not permit them to work on Sunday. Remonstrances and arguments were in vain, and we had to permit them to depart after exacting a promise that they would return early the next morning. Luka, the chief guide, lingered a while to state that his family burial place was beneath the great platform of Tongariki, and that he had a decided aversion to having the skulls of his ancestors added to our collection.

Sunday inspection and its attendant functions has through long custom become second nature with the men who have been long in the service, and through the desire to thus mark the day, the most valuable of our geological specimens were lost. The boatswain's mate took advantage of our temporary absence to clean up the cave and make it more presentable, and, in doing so, threw all the stones and "trash" into the sea. Nothing could be said, in view of the fact that it was done with the best possible intentions, but he was greatly chagrined to find that those same stones had been carried over many a weary mile to be lost now, when it was impossible to obtain duplicates or other specimens of some of the peculiar formations met with on the first days of the trip.

RANA RORAKA.

The day was devoted to the examination of the inside of the crater of Rana Roraka. The walls of the crater are very abrupt except on the west side, where the lava-flow escaped to the sea, and here the cattle and horses find easy access to the pool of water that has collected in the bottom. High up on the southern side are the workshops of the image-builders, extending in irregular terraces quite to the top. Here we found images in all stages of incompletion (Fig. 10), from the rude

FIG. 10.
UNFINISHED IMAGE, CRATER OF RANA RORAKA.

outline drawing to the finished statue ready to be cut loose from its original rock and launched down the steep incline. The *modus operandi* appears to have been to select a suitable rock upon which the image was sketched in a reclining position. The upper surface having been carved into shape and entirely finished, the last work was to cut the back loose from the rock. This necessitated the exercise of great care to prevent the breaking off of exposed portions, and was accomplished by building piles of stones to sustain the weight while it was being undermined.

Ninety-three statues in all, similar to those shown in Figs. 11 and 12, were counted inside the crater, and of these forty are standing up, completed and ready to be transported to the platforms for which they were

FIG. 11.
IMAGE: RANA RORAKA (front view.)

FIG. 12.
IMAGE: RANA RORAKA (back view.)

intended. They stand well down towards the bottom of the slope, and are more or less buried in the earth by the washings from above, as shown in Figs. 13 and 14.

The work of lowering the huge images from the upper terraces to the bottom of the crater and thence over the wall and down into the plain below, was of great magnitude, and we are lost in wonder that so much could be accomplished by rude savages ignorant of everything in the way of mechanical appliances. The average weight of these statues would be something between 10 and 12 tons, but some are very large and would weigh over 40 tons. It is possible that a slide was made, upon which the images were launched to the level ground below; a number of broken and damaged figures lie in a position to suggest that idea, but from the bottom of the crater they were transported up and over the wall and thence over hill and dale to various points all over the island. Excavations were made at different points inside the crater, but nothing was found of interest beyond a few broken stone implements that had no doubt been used by the image-builders.

Fig. 13. Buried Image: Crater of Rana Roraka.

Fig. 14. Image Standing Inside the Crater of Rana Roraka.

December 27.—We made an early start and visited the image-builders' workshops on the west side of Rana Roraka, which are much more extensive than those on the inside of the crater. These workshops commence well up on the side of the mountain and extend quite to the summit by irregular terraces. In places these terraces extend one above another with unfinished images upon each, and the configuration of the land is such as to preclude all idea of launching the statues by means of a slide. We were unable to arrive at any satisfactory conclusion as to how the immense statues on the upper tier of works could be moved to the plain below, passing over the underlying cavities where similar works had been quarried. We know the natives had ropes made of hemp, two kinds of which are indigenous to the island, but it is difficult to conjecture how these heavy weights were handled without mechanical appliances. One hundred and fifty-five images were counted upon this slope in various stages, including those standing at the base of the mountain finished and complete, ready for removal to the platforms. Many of the images in the workshops are of huge proportions, but the largest one on the island lies on one of the central terraces in an unfinished condition and measures 70 feet in length, 14½ feet across the body; the head being 28½ feet long. Some of the standing statues are in as perfect condition as the day they were finished.

One (Fig. 15) is noticeable from the fact that the head is slightly turned to one side and is known as the "wry-neck," but whether it is the result of accident or design could not be determined.

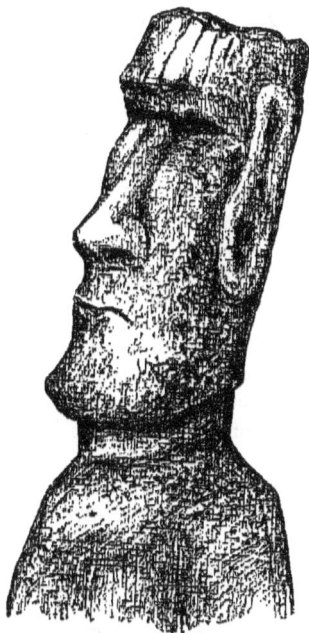

FIG. 15.
"WRY-NECK" IMAGE, RANA RORAKA.

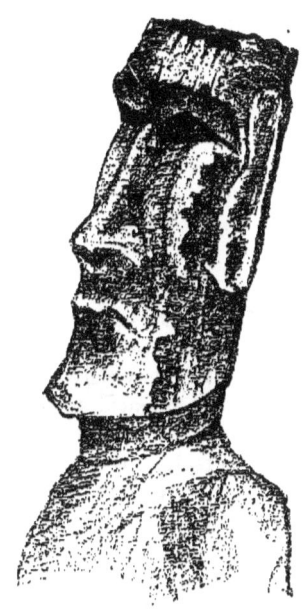

FIG. 16.
THE MUTILATED IMAGE "HIARA," OUTSIDE OF CRATER OF RANA RORAKA.

Another excellent specimen (Fig. 16) of these remarkable figures stands near the last mentioned and shows tool-marks around the neck as though an effort had been made to cut the head off. The natives call this "hiara" and have a tradition to the effect that it belonged to a powerful clan who were finally defeated in war, and that their enemies had made an attempt to destroy the statue by cutting off the head. The story may be based only upon the mutilation, but the chances are that it is founded upon fact.

Nothing of importance was found by digging about the images or in the workshops except broken stone implements which had been used by the builders. In one of the quarries we found the only trace of sculptured figures in the vicinity.

These emblems were carved upon a smooth rock over a half-finished image.

December 28.—Shortly after daylight the entire force started making excavations under the foundations of the image-builders houses, the ruins of which extend towards Rana Roraka from Tongariki Bay, on regular terraces. These peculiar ruins are to be found here in great numbers both inside and outside of the crater, but do not differ from those already described. A custom obtained among the islanders, similar to that practiced by the tribes of Alaska and other Indians of America, of burying something of interest or value beneath the doorposts of their dwellings. Usually it was a smooth beach pebble which was supposed to have some fetish qualities to bring good luck or ward off evil influences.

One of the largest of these ruins has an extensively paved terrace in front. At a depth of about three feet below the surface of the central doorway, we found a rough angular flinty stone with a rudely carved face upon it. A prominent ruin of the same description inside of the crater, and another near the workshop on the outside, yielded a hard stone upon which marks had been carved very similar to those on the rocks at Orongo.

SKULLS SHOWING PECULIAR MARKS.

One of our guides produced from a hiding place three ancient skulls, described elsewhere, upon the top of which these same mystical figures had been cut. They were not shown until a reward had been promised, and the guide claimed to have obtained them in their present condition from the King's platform.

On the outside of the crater of Rana Roraka, near the top and looking towards the southwest, we found a workshop containing fifteen small images. These had been overlooked in our former trips to this place.

Scattered over the plains extending towards Vaihu are a large number of images, all lying face downward. The indications are that they were being removed to their respective platforms when the work was suddenly arrested. These heavy weights were evidently moved by main strength, but why they were dragged over the ground face downward instead of upon their backs, thus protecting their features, is a mystery yet unsolved. One statue in a group of three is that of a female; the face and breast is covered with lichen, which at a short distance gives it the appearance of being whitewashed.

December 29.—We continued the work of exploration from Vaihu around the southwest points of the island. Excavations were made wherever the indications were good, but the results did not differ from those already described. Mount Orito was visited, from whence the obsidian was obtained for spear-heads, and also the quarries that produce the red pigment from which the natives make a red paint by rubbing it down with the juice of the sugar-cane. The remainder of the stay on Easter Island was devoted to the collection of traditions, translations of tablets, and similar matters of interest.

INSIDE THE CRATER OF RANA RORAKA, ON SLOPE BELOW THE ANCIENT WORKSHOPS.

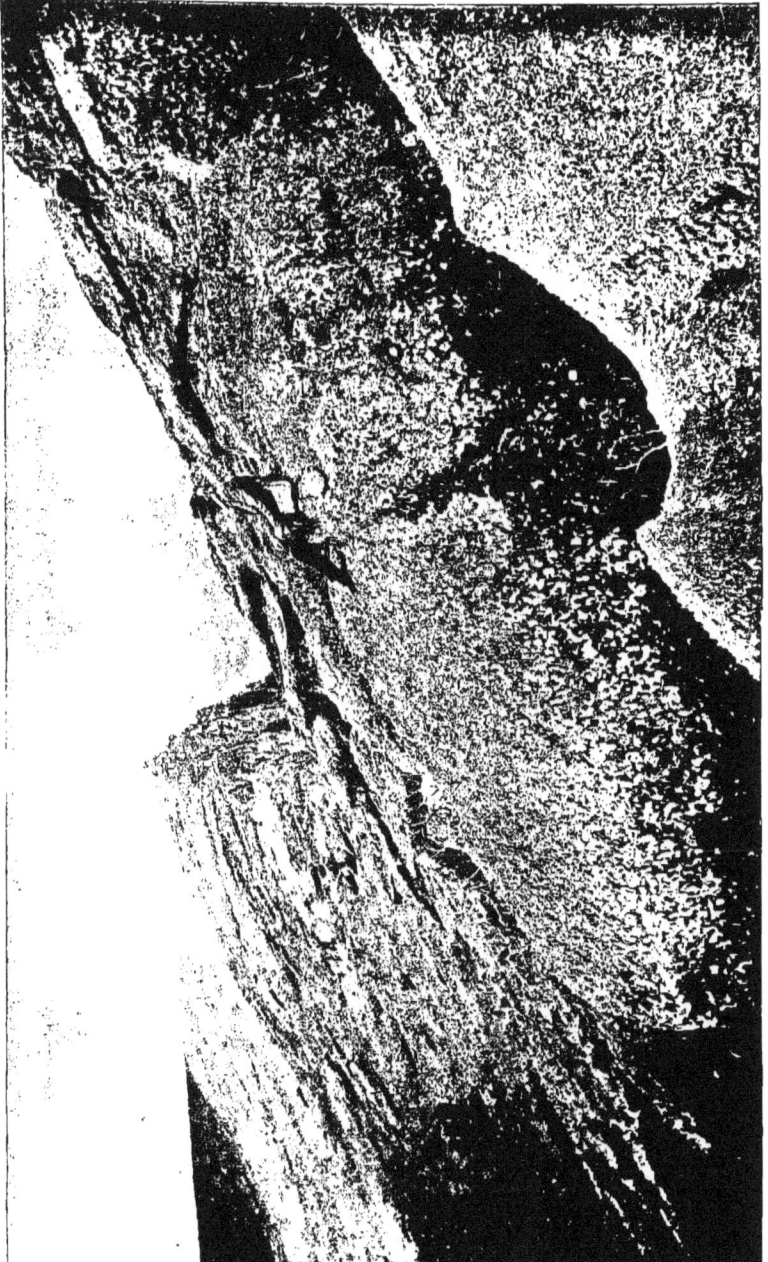

View of upper Workshops, on inner rim of Rana Roraka.

PLATFORMS AND IMAGES.

In order to form an estimate of the magnitude of the work performed by the image-makers, every one on the island was carefully counted, and the list shows a total of five hundred and fifty-five images (Plates XXV and XXVI). Of this number forty are standing inside of the crater and nearly as many more on the outside of Rana Roraka (Plate XXVII), at the foot of the slope where they were placed as finished and ready for removal to the different platforms for which they were designed; some finished statues lie scattered over the plains (Plate XXVIII) as though they were being dragged toward a particular locality but were suddenly abandoned. The large majority of the images, however, are lying near the platforms all around the coast, all more or less mutilated and some reduced to a mere shapeless fragment. Not one stands in its original position upon a platform. The largest image is in one of the workshops in an unfinished state and measures 70 feet in length; the smallest was found in one of the caves and is a little short of 3 feet in length. One of the largest images that has been in position lies near the platform which it ornamented, near Ovahe; it is 32 feet long and weighs 50 tons.

Images representing females were found. One at Anakena is called "Viri-viri Moai-a-Taka" and is apparently as perfect as the day it was finished; another, on the plain west of Rana Roraka is called "Moai Putu," and is in a fair state of preservation. The natives have names for every one of the images. The designation of images and platforms as obtained from the guides during the exploration was afterwards checked off in company with other individuals without confusion in the record. The coarse gray trachytic lava of which the images were made, is found only in the vicinity of Rana Roraka and was selected because the conglomerate character of the material made it easily worked with the rude stone implements that constituted the only tools possessed by the natives. The disintegration of the material when exposed to the action of the elements is about equivalent to that of sandstone under similar conditions, and admits of an estimate in regard to the probable age. The traditions in regard to the images are numerous, but relate principally to impossible occurrences, such as being endowed with power to walk about in the darkness, assisting certain clans by subtle means in contests, and delivering oracular judgments. The legends state that a son of King Mahuta Ariiki, named Tro Kaibo, designed the first image, but it is difficult to arrive at an estimation of the period. The journals of the early navigators throw but little light upon the subject. The workshops must have been in operation at the time of Captain Cook's visit, but unfortunately his exploration of the island was not directed towards the crater of Rana Roraka.

Although the images range in size from the colossus of 70 feet down to the pigmy of 3 feet, they are clearly all of the same type and general characteristics. The head is long, the eyes close under the heavy brows, the nose long, low-bridged, and expanded at the nostrils, the upper lip short and the lips pouting. The aspect is slightly upwards, and the expression is firm and profoundly solemn. Careful investigation failed to detect the slightest evidence that the sockets had ever been fitted with artificial eyes, made of bone and obsidian, such as are placed in the wooden images.

The head was in all cases cut flat on top to accommodate the red tufa crowns with which they were ornamented, but the images standing on the outside of the crater had flatter heads and bodies than those found around the coast. The images represent the human body only from the head to the hips, where it is cut squarely off to afford a good polygon of support when standing. The artists seem to have exhausted their talents in executing the features, very little work being done below the shoulders, and the arms being merely cut in low relief. The ears are only rectangular projections, but the lobes are represented longer in the older statues than in those of more recent date.

The images were designed as effigies of distinguished persons and intended as monuments to perpetuate their memory. They were never regarded as idols, and were not venerated or worshiped in any manner. The natives had their tutelary genii, gods, and goddesses, but they were represented by small wooden or stone idols, which bore no relation to the images that ornamented the burial platforms. The image-makers were a privileged class, and the profession descended from father to son. Some of the natives still claim a descent from the image-makers, and refer to their ancestors with as much pride as to the royal family. One of our guides never missed an opportunity of stating that one of his forefathers was Unrautahui, the distinguished image-maker.

The work of carving the image into shape and detaching it from the rock of which it was a part, did not consume a great deal of time, but the chief difficulty was, in the absence of mechanical contrivances, to launch it safely down the slope of the mountain and transport it to a distant point. It was lowered to the plain by a system of chocks and wedges, and the rest was a dead drag accomplished by main strength. A roadway was constructed, over which the images were dragged by means of ropes made of indigenous hemp, and sea-weed and grass made excellent lubricants. The platforms were all built with sloping terraces in the rear, and up this incline a temporary road-way was constructed of a suitable height, upon which the statue could be rolled until the base was over its proper resting-place. The earth was then dug away to allow the image to settle down into position, the ropes being used to steady it in the mean time. It was a work of great magnitude, but we can clearly see how it was accomplished with a large force of able-bodied men.

The crowns, or head ornaments, were made of red vesicular tufa, quarried in the Teraai Hills, where many finished specimens are still standing.

IMAGES STANDING AT THE BASE OF OUTER SLOPE OF RANA RORAKA.

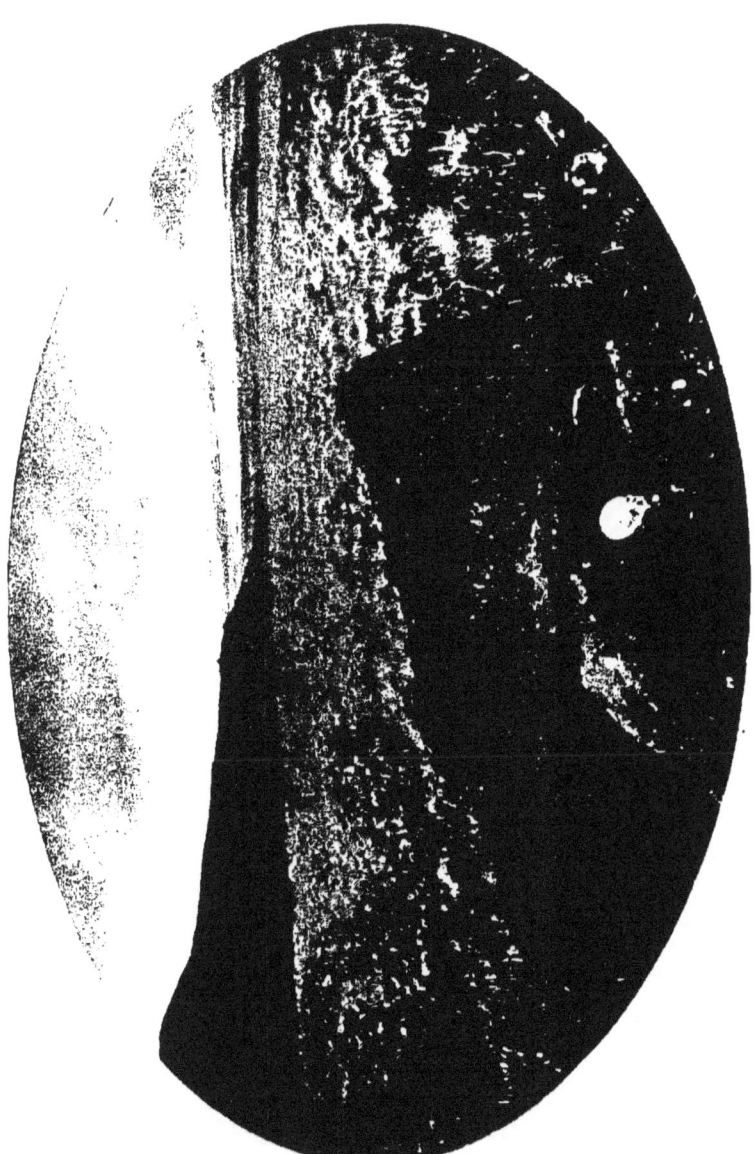

PLAIN OF ANAKENA.

The image in the foreground is now in the National Museum

(Cat. No. 129308, U. S. N. M. Easter Island. Collected by Paymaster W. J. Thomson, U. S. N.)

These truncated cones, nearly cylindrical in shape, were easily transported. The material is readily quarried and fashioned, being light, only about 1.4 times heavier than water, while the average density of the image-stone is about 2.1.

The largest crown measured was $12\frac{1}{2}$ feet in diameter, but of those that had actually been placed in position the average weight would not be more than 3 tons. The crowns were placed in position upon the heads of the standing images by building a road-way upon which they could be rolled to the proper spot. The clearing away of the incline was the final act. The earth which formed the surface was utilized as garden-patches, and the stones which formed the foundation of the roadway were disposed of in building the wing-extensions of the platform. The platforms differ greatly in dimensions, but the general plan and characteristics are invariably the same. Many of them are in a fair state of preservation, except that the images have been thrown down and the terraces in the rear obliterated or strewn with rubbish, while others have been reduced to a state of complete ruin. The platforms are usually located near the beach, and on the high bluff some of them are quite near the edge, overlooking the sea. The general plan consists of a front elevation composed of blocks of stone fairly well squared and neatly fitted together without cement, a parallel wall forming the inside boundary, built of uncut stone, inclosing small chambers or tombs placed at irregular intervals. Loose bowlders fill the spaces between the tombs and form the horizontal plane of the platform, into which are let the rectangular stones which constituted the base upon which the images stood. The façade stones are large and heavy, and in some cases the smooth surface presented could not well be attributed to the rude implements at the command of the builders, and must have been produced by friction or grinding. Long wings composed of uncut stone extend from the platform proper, built up to the summit at the line of junction and sloping away to the surface of the ground at the ends. In the rear of the platform a few steps descend to a gently sloping terrace, which terminates in a low wall and is bounded by a squarely built wall raised above the ground so as to join the top of the platform. Human remains fill the inner chambers, and bones lie scattered about among the loose bowlders of the platform and its extensions. The ruined condition of these solid specimens of architecture, with the overthrown images and immense deposit of loose bowlders on the surface of the ground, are strongly suggestive of earthquakes and volcanic eruption. The images in all stages of incompletion in the workshops, and abandoned *en route* to the coast in various directions, indicate that the work was suddenly arrested, and not gradually brought to an end; but the traditions are silent upon the subject, and no record has been handed down of the disturbance of any of the volcanoes on the island.

Platform No. 1.—Known to the natives as "Hanga Roa". Only the base remains, measuring 59 feet long by 7 feet wide. This pile was demolished to obtain material for the construction of a house for one of the Catholic missionaries formerly stationed on the island.

Platform No. 2.—Called "Ana Koiroraroa"; 160 feet long by 12½ feet wide and 10 feet high. The facing-stones on the front line remain intact, but the body of the platform is a mere mass of loose stones, probably torn up by the natives in recent years for the purpose of depositing their dead in these ancient structures. The three statues that formerly adorned this pile are lying immediately in the rear, and show from their positions that they had faced inboard, with their backs to the sea. These images are much weather-worn and defaced: one is entire; another has the head lying close by, probably broken off in the fall; and the third is minus the head and with the neck showing saw-marks. We afterwards found out that a French vessel of war visited the island a few years ago and the head of this image was cut off by them and taken to Europe.

Platform No. 3 (See Fig. 17).—Called "Hanga Varevare"; 50 feet long and 8 feet wide. This has the appearance of an unfinished pile and is merely a burial place covered with loose rocks and without the usual smoothly faced stones in front. We found the catacombs or tombs underneath this platform had been robbed of the most ancient skulls, and concluded that the Frenchmen had taken everything of interest away.

Platform No. 3, Image Restored.
Fig. 17.
Hanga Varevare.

Platform No. 4.—Called "Tahai"; 160 feet long, 7½ feet wide, and 7 feet high. In a bad state of preservation, but the facing-stones on the front are sufficiently plain, while the rest of the pile is a mass of loose stones. Five large flat stones at regular intervals along the platform, show where the images once stood. The statues have fallen face downward on the inshore side, and are much broken and dilapidated. The one on the north end is of gigantic size, and much larger than the others. The red tufa crown that adorned this image lies near it, and measures 7 feet 9 inches wide; 5 feet 9 inches in ellipse; and 4 feet 9 inches high, and the top is ornamented by sculptured lines that have the appearance of geometrical figures, but are too much obliterated to decipher.

Platform No. 5.—Called by the same name as the last, only a few yards distant, is shaped like a right angle, and it is possible that these two platforms may have been originally designed for one of huge proportions. The stones of which it is composed have been thrown about in such disorder that the original design can not be followed, but the flat base stones indicate where the images once stood. At one end of this platform a statue 14 feet high and 9 feet across the hips, lies face downward on the inboard side, and at the other end, one measuring 15 feet long and 6 feet wide, lies face downward toward the sea, being one of the few images on the island found in that position, admitting the possibility of having faced outboard.

Platform No. 6.—Called "Anotai"; 120 feet long, 17½ feet wide, and 7½ feet high. In a bad state of preservation, though the faced stones on the front may be traced. The remains of one image lies on the inboard side, but minus the head. A large cavity in the center of the back of this image attracted attention, but could not be explained. The red tufa crown belonging to this statue lies half-buried in the earth, about 100 feet distant. Under the center of this platform were obtained some interesting relics, and the tombs bore evidence of great antiquity.

Platform No. 7.—Called "Ahuakapu"; 101 feet long, 9 feet wide, and 8 feet high. In a bad state of preservation. Three images lying on the front side with the appearance of having been pulled over backwards, and one upon the inshore side down upon its face. All four statues are in good condition, except that the heads have been broken off at the neck by the fall. One of these detached heads measured 5 feet 3 inches in length by 3 feet 2 inches from ear to ear. The four pedestal stones are still in place on the platform and average 4 feet long and 3 feet 8 inches wide, and are composed of hard volcanic rock, roughly squared.

Platform No. 8.—Called "Anaoraka"; 95 feet long and 8 feet wide and 7 feet high. Remarkable for the large stones that support the sea face, the largest of which measures 6 feet 9 inches high and 4 feet 7 inches wide. Four images have fallen upon their faces upon the inboard side. Only a pedestal stone remains in position, which is 5 feet 2 inches square by 2 feet 2 inches thick. (Fig. 18).

Platform No. 9.—Called "Kihikihiraumea"; 186 feet long, 8 feet 10 inches wide, and 7 feet 5 inches thick. The central section of this structure contains stones so remarkably well cut and fitted ogether that it merits the accompanying sketch. Four images were found, which had been thrown down on their faces on the inboard side. These are in a fair state of preservation. From this ruin we obtained skulls, obsidian spear-heads, and stone tools.

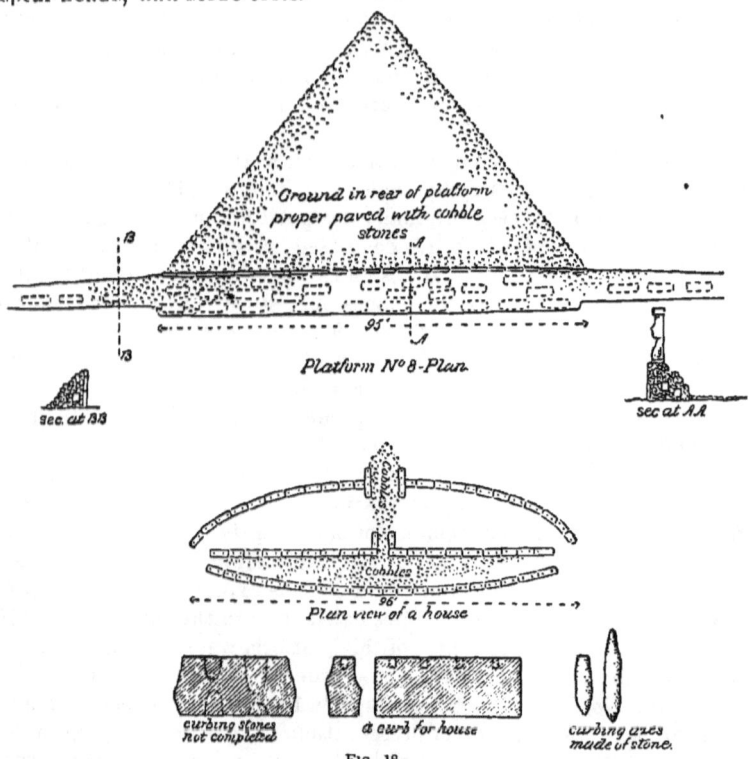

FIG. 18.
SHOWING GENERAL PLAN OF CONSTRUCTION OF PLATFORM. ALSO PLAN OF HOUSE CONSTRUCTION WITH DETAILS.

Platform No. 10.—Called "Ahutepeu". Is in such a state of dilapidation that it was impossible to obtain accurate measurements. Portions of an image are here, but it looks as though others might have been rolled over the edge of the cliff, which is only a few feet distant and about 450 feet high, and against the base of which the sea dashes incessantly.

Platform No. 11.—Called "Hanauakou". Central sections 48 feet long, 12 feet wide, and 9 feet high; total length, with wings, 248 feet. This is an exceedingly fine platform, and contains some remarkably large stones. In the face of the main structure are huge blocks of igneous rock that appear to have once been fashioned into faces and figures, but now so destroyed by the action of the elements and perhaps by the hand of the iconoclast that the features can only be dimly traced. Hard work with

"OHAU" PLATFORM, NO. 12, SHOWING PECULIARLY FITTED STONES. CENTER STONE WEIGHS 6 TONS; CIRCULAR PEDESTAL STONE, 5½ FEET IN DIAMETER.

our entire force disclosed beneath this platform well constructed catacombs and tombs, containing human remains so old that they crumbled into dust upon exposure to the air. The removal of one of the facing-stones revealed a lot of skulls with remarkably broad, heavy underjaws. These were generally too brittle to be handled, and a peculiar feature about the find was the fact that these heads had been entombed together, and the surroundings excluded the idea of any other portions of the bodies having been interred with them. Only one image is in sight, and the proximity of the platform to the edge of the bluff suggests the possibility that other statues may have been thrown into the sea. From the size and character of the work on the structure it is not reasonable to suppose that it was designed to support the one insignificant statue that lies near it.

Platform No. 12.—Called "Ohau". Central section 18 feet long, 9 feet wide, and 6 feet high. One image thrown down upon its face on the inboard side, 8 feet 4 inches long; extreme width of body 5 feet; length of head 4 feet; and width from ear to ear, 3 feet 3 inches. Good state of preservation. (Plate XXIX).

Platform No. 13.—Called "Ahukinokino". In such a state of ruin that measurements were not obtainable. Situated close to the edge of the high cliff.

Platform No. 14.—Called "Ahutoretore". Has been so completely destroyed that nothing can be determined about its original size and importance. Excavations in this vicinity produced nothing but a few stray spear heads of obsidian.

Platform No. 15.—Called "Haugatariri"; 103 feet long, 11 feet wide; and 6 feet high. In very bad condition, but some of the large cut facing-stones are in position. Four images lie face downward on the island side, and two more have fallen on their backs toward the sea. A few yards back of this structure is a tomb 50 feet long and 6 feet wide, built of stones taken from the platform and those peculiarly cut stones that form the foundations of the image-builders' houses. At one end is a hard stone slab that appears to have been covered with hieroglyphics, but they are too nearly obliterated to be accurately traced. After a thorough investigation we concluded that it was of comparatively recent date and had no distinctive features of its own. On the plain, a few hundred yards distant, is an image of gigantic proportions lying upon its face with the head toward the sea. The indications are that it was designed for this platform and was being moved into position when from some sudden emergency it had to be abandoned. The ground underneath the statue has been dug out by later generations in such a manner that the body of the image forms the roof of the cave. The base of the statue shows traces of rudely sculptured figures, nearly obliterated. In this vicinity are several large caves, with the narrow entrances completely blocked up with loose stones, which were not investigated for the want of time.

Platform No. 16.—Called "Haugaoteo"; 70 feet long and 12 feet wide. Has the appearance of having been in process of construction when the work was suddenly suspended.

Platform No. 17.—Called "Tumuheipara"; 40 feet long, 8 feet wide, and 8 feet high. This structure also appears to have been abandoned before completion. The chances are that several days could have been spent upon the extensive plain, back of these images, to great advantage and it is regretted that the limited time at our disposal did not allow a more thorough investigation.

Platform No. 18.—Called "Haahuroa". Central section 40 feet long, 12 feet wide, and 7 feet high, with wings 145 feet in length. One image lying on the inboard side measures 7 feet 5 inches long and 3 feet 5 inches wide; length of head to shoulders 3 feet 4 inches, and width from ear to ear 3 feet 5 inches. The fragments of two other images lie in front of the platform. The huge facing-stones of this structure have been thrown about as though by some great convulsion of nature, and some of them bear evidences of having been ornamented with sculptured figures.

Platform No. 19.—Called "Akane". Seems to have been abandoned while in the process of construction. A few faced stones intended for the front of the central section are lying about, but were never placed in position.

Platform No. 20.—Called "Ahuroa". Is a mere mass of loose rocks, said to have been destroyed in the tribal wars, but it has the appearance of having never been completed.

Platform No. 21.—Called "Vaiavaugarenga". In the same condition as the last. No images.

Platform No. 22.—Called "Maiki". Same as the last; merely a pile of loose stones covering human remains. These platforms may have been robbed to supply the material for the construction of the numerous houses and cairns, the ruins of which cover the hills in this vicinity.

Platform No. 23.—Called "Tauka". Central section 38 feet long, 48 feet wide, and 12 feet high, the extreme length with wings 120 feet. In very bad condition. One small image lies face-upward toward the sea, much broken. Facing and other suitable stones have been removed from this platform for the construction of tombs and houses. Near at hand is one of those peculiar ways, made by paving the sloping bank with regular lines of smooth, round bowlders, as though intended for hauling up heavy boats or weights.

Platform No. 24.—Called "Punamuta". In its incipient stage, and important only from the fact that it shows the manner of laying the foundation of the work.

Platform No. 25.—Called "Koteva". This has been an important structure and was built in the shape of a right angle 60 feet long, 11 feet wide, and 20 feet high. Portions of the walls have been thrown down, and no images could be found.

Platform No. 26.—Called "Tetonga". Similar in shape and structure to the last, but of smaller size. From these piles we obtained relics in the shape of obsidian spear-heads, stone implements, and skulls.

Platform No. 27.—Called "Hanghaogio"; 150 feet long, 8 feet wide, and 10 feet high. Three small images have been thrown down and much broken.

Platform No. 28.—Called "Huarero". Very similar to the last, but located on the hill-side about three-quarters of a mile back of the bay. The facing-stones show traces of carving, but so nearly obliterated that only these figures could be made out: ⌒, ⌘, and they seemed to be often repeated. The fragments of two images lie behind the platform.

Platform No. 29.—Called "Anakena"; 75 feet long, 8 feet wide, and 10 feet high. An image lies upon its face upon the inboard side, 13 feet long and 9 feet across the hips; length of head, to shoulders, 5 feet, and width, from ear to ear, 6 feet 6 inches. This image is in the best state of preservation of any found about the platforms of the island. The traditions state that it was the last statue finished and set up in place. Our guides maintained that this is the statue of a female, and that it was only thrown down about twenty-four years ago. Its size, and proximity to the perfectly smooth landing place at Anakena Bay, would insure its easy removal to a vessel. From the sand beach at Anakena Bay we passed over hills composed of volcanic cinder as light as coke, but very hard. Beyond this are numerous ruins of houses, each with a small stone building connected that was evidently designed for fowls. The largest of these was about 8 feet square, and the only opening was a small hole for the chickens to pass through.

Platform No. 30.—Called "Abutrature". Central section 30 feet long, 10 feet wide, and 6 feet high. Extreme length 80 feet. In ruins, with no images.

Platform No. 31.—Called "Anateka"; 30 feet long, 12 feet wide, and 7 feet high. Extreme length 100 feet. In a very bad condition. Small fragments are all that remain of two images and two crowns.

Platform No. 32.—Called "Ahupuapuatetea". Merely a shapeless mass of uncut stones remain to indicate the site of the structure.

Platform No. 33.—Called "Ahangakihikihi"; 20 feet long, 10 feet wide, and 9 feet high. In ruins. One small image lies on the inboard side in a bad condition.

Platform No. 34.—Called "Puuahoa". Although in ruins, this has evidently been a structure of some importance; 175 feet long, 8 feet wide, with the central section projecting 6 feet forward of the main line. The facing-stones are from 6 feet to 9 feet in length by 5 feet and 1 foot in thickness. An image lies upon its face on the inboard side, and measures 32 feet long, 10 feet 3 inches wide; length of head, to shoulders, 12 feet and 6 inches. Near this platform we found a peculiar stone nearly buried in the earth. After much digging it proved to be nearly spherical in shape and about 8 feet 4 inches in circumference. The natives called it "Petakula", and we could only make out that it was a grinding stone of some sort.

Platform No. 35.—Called "Puapau"; 150 feet long, 10 feet wide, and 8 feet high, with a small platform in front of it. The building of this elaborate structure must have furnished employment for a large number of people. The foundation stones are of hard rock of immense size, all smoothly faced. Four images have been thrown down, two on each side, and all much broken.

Platform No. 36.—Called "Hangakouri". Central section 70 feet long, 7 feet wide, and 8 feet high. Extreme length 300 feet. In a state of absolute ruin and no images.

Platform No. 37.—Called "Hangabohoonu". Completely in ruins and with one image in a bad condition. Between these last two platforms is a paved way leading to a small channel through the rocks that affords a safe and convenient landing for small boats.

Platform No. 38.—Called "Mari". Central section 80 feet long, 12 feet wide, and 7 feet high. Extreme length 300 feet, situated very close to edge of the bluff.

Platform No. 39.—Called "Ahurai". Very large; but, like the last, in a state of ruin.

Platform No. 40.—Called "Tehahitunukiolaira". Of great size; but, like the last, in a state of absolute ruin; covering human remains.

Platform No. 41.—Called "Narnaanga". Small and inferior; also in ruins and no images.

Platform No. 42—Called "Haugaopuna"; 100 feet long and 10 feet wide. Has two layers of roughly cut stones in the front face, and appears to have been left in an unfinished state.

Platform No. 43.—Called "Tumatuma"; 25 feet long, 7 feet wide, and 7 feet high. Poorly constructed, and contains nothing of interest but one small image.

Platform No. 44.—Called "Tokaie". Larger than the last, but in a bad condition. A much battered head lies just behind the pile, but the rest of the image can not be found.

Platform No. 45.—Called "Vaimangeo"; 50 feet long, 8 feet wide, and 15 feet high. Extreme length, including wings, 150 feet. In a state of ruin, and has one large image thrown down on the inboard side.

Platform No. 46.—Called "Moukuhoi"; 20 feet long, 7 feet wide, and 5 feet high. Extreme length, including wings, 60 feet. Situated very close to the edge of the bluff, and looks as if the destroyers of the structure might have tossed the most of it into the sea.

Platform No. 47.—Called "Moukuroa". In all respects a duplicate of the last one.

Platform No. 48.—Called "Motuariki"; 20 feet long, 7 feet wide, and 5 feet high. Extreme length, including wings, 260 feet. This has been a large and imposing structure. The central section, upon which the im-

Central Section of the Great Platform of Tongariki.

RIGHT WING OF PLATFORM OF TONGARIKI. BROKEN IMAGE ON PEDESTAL; THE ONLY ONE ON THE ISLAND FOUND IN ITS ORIGINAL POSITION ON A PLATFORM.

LEFT WING OF PLATFORM OF TONGARIKI.

REAR VIEW OF RIGHT WING OF PLATFORM OF TONGARIKI, SHOWING FALLEN IMAGES.

Rear View of Central Section of Platform of Tongariki, with fallen Images.

age stood projects beyond the line of the platform, and was higher. In the rear, and extending the entire length of the pile, is a broad terrace, neatly paved with smooth round bowlders. The fragments of three images lie upon the terrace.

Platform No. 49.—Called "Oneonepuhea". Centralsection is about 45 feet long by 6 feet high. This is a crescent-shaped structure, and the only one of the kind that we saw on the island. It is situated on the extreme edge of the cliff, which at this point has a straight-away fall of over 500 feet to the sea, which dashes against its wall-like base. There is no image in sight, but a large pedestal stone, inclined at a sharp angle towards the sea, shows where one has stood and suggests what became of it.

Platform No. 50.—Called "Abutakaure". Located on Poike cliff, facing westward; is small and unimportant and in a state of complete ruin. On the east slope of the mountain we found an image, the head of which had been broken off, but it lies near by. There is no platform here and no indications that one was intended to be built in the vicinity; so we concluded that the statue was being moved to some distant locality when it was broken and abandoned.

Platform No. 51.—Called "Hangaiti"; 30 feet long and 8 feet wide and 5 feet high. In a bad condition and one small image broken.

Platform No. 52.—Called "Tongariki"; 150 feet long, 9 feet wide, and 8 feet high (Plates XXX–XXXIV). Extreme length, including original wings, 540 feet. This is the largest platform on the island, and was ornamented with fifteen gigantic statues. These have been thrown down upon their faces on the inshore side, and the most of these are broken, the one on the south end being fractured across the middle of the body, leaving the lower section still standing. The red tufa crowns are lying a short distance away and are also much broken. The hard stones of which the sea-front of this platform is constructed are of immense size, faced and neatly joined together. One of the foundation-stones in the center of this wall is of red tufa and represents a human head.

Our investigations were commenced at this point by throwing down the facing-stones and working straight backwards through the platform. The labor was great, and occupied the most of our force for nearly two days, but the catacombs and tombs underlying the structure were thoroughly examined. Under the central section are small, narrow passages forming a part of the original design, having been built up while the platform was in process of construction, and containing human remains. The oldest of these tombs appear to have been sealed up before the structure was completed, and the probability is that they were not intended to be opened, from the fact that there is nothing to indicate their exact locality. The pedestal-stones, all of which are still in place, show that the images were put up at equal distances and with a view to symmetry, and without regard to the position of the tombs; though it is pretty well established that they were intended as effigies of chiefs or distinguished persons. The terrace behind the platform was also used as a burial-place, and contained remains of an ancient date. Succeeding generations have utilized the same places for the same purposes, but there are passages under the platform that have never been opened since the structure was built. The entire plain back of Tongariki Bay is one vast cemetery, containing the decaying remains of thousands of people. Every pile of stones, cave or ruined platform, house or cairn, has been used as a tomb. The christianized natives of to-day still regard this as a favorite burial-place. They have neither the ambition nor the industry to construct tombs for themselves, but are content to place their dead in receptacles filled with the remains of their ancestors. The recess-angles between the bodies of the fallen images, and the platforms upon which the base rests, are filled with remains of a recent date.

Platform No. 53.—Called "One-tea". Completely in ruins. Three images much broken. Foundation proper about 100 feet long.

Platform No. 54.—Called "Opaarionga". Small and unimportant. Central section 20 feet long, 6 feet wide, and 7 feet high. Remains of one small image.

Platform No. 55.—Called "Hangatufata"; 125 feet long, 8 feet wide, and 7 feet high. Five images thrown down, broken and in bad condition.

Platform No. 56.—Called "Onemakihi". Central section 40 feet long, 7 feet wide, and 7 feet high. Extreme length, including wings, 100 feet. One image much mutilated.

Platform No. 57.—Called "Puuakape". Central section 40 feet long, 6 feet wide, and 6 feet high. Extreme length 80 feet. In ruins, and no images.

Platform No. 58.—Called "Moaitutahi". Central section 150 feet long, 7 feet wide, and 7 feet high. Extreme length 250 feet. Only two images remain, but appearances indicate that others have been destroyed. Upon terraces sloping towards the sea from the front are numerous remains of image-builders' houses. From the back of the structure a nicely paved way, 10 feet wide, extends inland for a distance of 200 yards.

Platform No. 59.—Called "Hanga-mahihiku". A mere mass of ruins, and almost devoid of shape. No images.

Platform No. 60.—Called "Ahuakoi". Central section 75 feet long, 7 feet wide, and 6 feet high. Extreme length, 160 feet. In a bad condition, and no images.

Platform No. 61.—Called "Hanga-tutuki". A mere mass of ruins covering human remains.

Platform No. 62.—Called "Ahupoepoe". In same condition as the last and without images.

Platform No. 63.—Called "Vaimoai". Central section 40 feet long, 6 feet wide, and 8 feet high. Extreme length, 90 feet. In bad condition, and no images.

AKAHANGA (KING'S PLATFORM), NO. 80, REAR VIEW.

Platform No. 64.—Called "Kai". Same dimensions and general appearance as the last, but has one broken image.

Platform No. 65.—Called "Ruruoa". Central section 150 feet long, 7 feet wide, and 6 feet high. Extreme length, including wings, 275 feet. Two large images, each 33 feet in length by 5 wide. Length of head, to shoulders, 10 feet, and width, from ear to ear, 4 feet. The stones on the front wall of the structure are neatly squared and smoothly faced.

Platform No. 66.—Called "Mahatua". Central section 30 feet long, 7 feet wide, and 6 feet high. Extreme length, 100 feet. Two images, much defaced, lie on the inboard side on their faces. Between this platform and the last there is a nicely graded and paved road, with gentle slope from the cliff to the water-edge.

Platform No. 67.—Called "Ahukirirera". Has been pretty well demolished. No images.

Platform No. 68.—Called "Tehangakiri". Central section 40 feet long, 7 feet wide, and 7 feet high. Extreme length, 250 feet. Here are seven images, three large ones and four small-sized, all in a damaged condition.

Platform No. 69.—Called "Kirikiriroa". Has been pretty thoroughly demolished, and has the fragments of one image.

Platform No. 70.—Called "Onepuhea". A duplicate of the last one in all respects.

Platform No. 71.—Called "Hanga-tetera"; 60 feet long, 6 feet wide, and 7 feet high, and has no wings. The main stones of sea-face average in size 5½ feet long and 1½ feet wide. No images.

Platform No. 72.—Called "Hanga-rea". Has been completely demolished and the fragments of two images lie among the ruins.

Platform No. 73.—Called "Oteu". Has a small foundation and seems to have been abandoned in an unfinished condition.

Platform No. 74.—Called "Tahureue". Has been destroyed, and the fragments of two images lie in the ruins.

Platform No. 75.—Called "Oroi". Central section 40 feet long, 6 feet wide, and 6 feet high. Extreme length, 140 feet. In a bad condition and no images.

Platform No. 76.—Called "Ahukinokino". Somewhat smaller than the last, but destitute of all interest.

Platform No. 77.—Called "Papaturei". A duplicate of the last, and in a demolished condition.

Platform No. 78.—Called "Tutuira". A mere mass of ruins, and with no images.

Platform No. 79.—Called "Ue". Central section 30 feet long, 6 feet wide, 6 feet high. Extreme length, 120 feet. Two images in a bad condition.

Platform No. 80.—Called "Akahanga." (Plate XXXV). Two hundred and fifty feet long, 10 feet wide, and 7 feet high, with no wings.

Thirteen colossal images that once ornamented this remarkable structure have been thrown down and more or less damaged. Their red tufa crowns, also considerably broken, lie near at hand. On the inland facing-wall there is a ground tier of gray volcanic stone finely dressed, and on this is a tier of tufa stones 4½ feet long, 2½ feet high, and 8 inches thick each, and these are covered with hieroglyphics. This is known as the King's platform, and is regarded as one of the most important on the island, on account of the finished work on the structure as well as the numerous sculptures (Fig. 19). The tradition

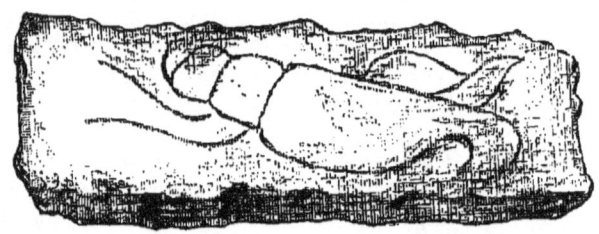

FIG. 19.
SCULPTURED ROCK: KING'S PLATFORM.

asserts that this was the burial place of Hotu-Matua, the first king, and a long line of his descendants. Our excavations in the vicinity produced nothing of interest beyond a few ancient skulls with lower jaws of extraordinary size and width. From the foundation of image-builders' houses we obtained fine stone implements and carving tools.

Platform No. 81.—Called "Harerora". Small and unimportant. One image, much broken.

Platform No. 82.—Called "Motnopope". Central section 252 feet long, 10 feet wide, and 7 feet high. Extreme length, 375 feet. Six images in rather bad condition. This structure is important from the fact that the statues have short ears, the only ones of the kind we found on the island. The sketches will show that on all the platforms, as well the images in the workshops as those left in an unfinished state were all carved with long ears. Why there was an exception made to the general rule in the images that adorned this structure, could not be determined.

Platform No. 83.—Called "Anaonero". Consisting of foundation stones only, showing that the work was abandoned shortly after being commenced.

Platform No. 84.—Called "Huareva". A mere mass of ruins.

Platform No. 85.—Called "Hoekoe". Has been completely demolished and shows fragments of two large images.

Platform No. 86.—Called "Pakaea". Central section 45 feet long, 8 feet wide, and 7 feet high, with wings extending 250 feet on either side. One image, in a bad condition.

Platform No. 87.—Called "Manumea". A mere mass of ruins.
Platform No. 88.—Called "Hanga-tee". Same condition as the last.
Platform No. 89. - Called "Kope-iti". Only the foundation-stones in place; probably never finished.
Platform No. 90.—Called "Runga-vae". Same condition as last.
Platform No. 91.—Called "Kote-one". In same unfinished state.
Platform No. 92.—Called "Renga-havini". A mere mass of ruins.
Platform No. 93.—Called "Kote-ara-ara". In a complete state of ruin.
Platform No. 94.—Called "Puepan". In same condition as the last.
Platform No. 95.—Called "Kiraau". A shapeless ruin.
Platform No. 96.—Called "Taroe". Central section 200 feet long, 8 feet wide, and 6½ feet high. Extreme length, 350 feet. Eleven images, all mutilated.
Platform No. 97.—Called "Ariki-iki". A shapeless ruin.
Platform No. 98.—Called "Kone-iti". Same condition as the last.
Platform No. 99.—Called "Koturara". In a very bad condition, with one broken image.
Platform No. 100.—Called "Moturea". In a state of absolute ruin.
Platform No. 101.—Called "Hanga-paukura". Shows that it was originally well built, and has six images lying behind it.
Platform No. 102.—In a very bad condition, and the name could not be ascertained.
Platform No. 103.—Called "Mataakira". A shapeless mass of ruins.
Platform No. 104.—Called "Auokahi". Similar to the last.
Platform No. 105.—Called "Hanga-hahne". In a bad condition, but has been an extensive structure with long wings. Four images.
Platform No. 106.—Called "Tehuteaheru". A mass of ruins.
Platform No. 107.—Called "Ahumeamea". Small and irregular construction. One image much damaged.
Platform No. 108.—Called "Ahumata-iti". This structure has been pretty thoroughly demolished and shows the fragments of one image.
Platform No. 109.—Called "Tahiri". The dimensions of the structure are not great, but it is remarkable on account of the finished workmanship. The sea front is built of immense blocks of hard heavy volcanic rock, smoothly faced and neatly joined together. In places, small stones have been mortised into the larger ones. It is surprising that such results could be produced by the rude stone implements that are known to have been the only tools at the command of the natives. Finished surfaces might be the result of grinding with sand and water, but the joints and fittings could only be accomplished by long and patient labor. Some of the facing-stones were estimated at a weight of upwards of 5 tons. Under the impression that the superior character of the work indicated a platform of more than usual importance, it was thoroughly investigated at the expense of great labor and time. A section of the front wall was thrown down and the stones removed

until an opening was made clear through the structure. No results having been obtained except a knowledge of how the pile was constructed from the foundation up, additional efforts were directed towards the two ends. To our great disappointment, we had nothing to show for the great labor expended upon this platform. The only human remains about the place are those of recent date, in shallow tombs on the rear side of the pile. There is a tradition to the effect that this was the last platform built on the island and was intended for the colossal image (70 feet) lying in the workshops on the west side of the crater of Rana Roraka. The legend asserts that when the work upon the platform and images had arrived at a certain stage, a great feast was held in honor of the event by the powerful tribe of Vinapu. The wife of the chief was of the Tongariki clan and during the ceremonies this "lady" was slighted in the division of "long pig," but whether intentionally or otherwise does not appear. Cannibalism was practiced on the island down to the advent of the first missionaries, and was always an important feature of the ancient feasts. The bodies were roasted in ovens made of hot stones covered with earth, after the manner practiced all through Polynesia, and certain portions were awarded to prominent individuals. Upon this particular occasion the rib-roast, "tenderloin" steak, or whatever the favorite morsel was which belonged to the aforesaid female by reason of her rank, was given to another. The insulted individual immediately sought the protection of her own clan, who arose *en masse* to vindicate the Tongariki honor. Long and bloody wars followed. Image-builders and platform-makers were drawn into the conflict from all parts of the island and, in a spirit of revenge, platforms were destroyed and images thrown down whenever opportunity offered. This is believed to have been the origin of the trouble which has laid waste the extraordinary works of this island.

Fig. 20.
Platform 110. "Vinapu."

Platform No. 110.—Called "Vinapu" (Fig. 20). A large structure with six mutilated images, and of the same general character and appearance as those already described. Immediately behind this platform a wall of earth incloses a piece of ground about 225 feet in diameter and circular in shape. This is believed to have been the theater of the native ceremonies, and perhaps the spot where the feasts were held. We made excavations in the center and around the sides, but without a "find."

Platform No. 111.—Called "Ahutupai." Has been pretty thoroughly demolished. Six images in a bad condition lie on the top of the pile.

Platform No. 112.—Called "Ahurikiriki." Situated on the extreme southwestern end of the island, and remarkable from its position on the face of a perpendicular cliff nearly 1,000 feet high and midway between the sea and the top. Sixteen small images are lying on this platform and many of them seem to be in excellent condition. We could find no way of reaching the narrow ledge upon which this platform stands. No road leads down from the top; it can not be approached from either side, and from below it is a straight up and down wall against which the sea dashes continually. It is hardly probable that the images were lowered from the top by ropes, and the natural conclusion is, that a roadway once existed, which has been undermined by the waves and has fallen into the sea.

Platform No. 113.—Called "Kaokaoe." This was originally a large structure, but has been completely demolished by Mr. Brander to obtain material for the construction of stone-fences about his place.

LANGUAGE.

The principal feature of interest, connected with Easter Island, is the written language by which the ancient traditions and legends were perpetuated. The existence of the incised tablets was not known until the missionaries settled upon the island. Numerous specimens were found in the possession of the natives, but no especial attention appears to have been directed towards them. Several persons, belonging to vessels that were wrecked at Easter Island, report having seen these tablets, but they were so highly prized by the natives, that they could not be induced to part with them. The three hundred islanders who emigrated to Tahiti had in their possession a number of these tablets; they created some attention on account of the remarkable skill with which the figures were executed, but they were highly prized by the owners and no effort was made to secure them because their real value was not discovered. The Chilian corvette *O'Higgins* visited Easter Island in January, 1870, and Captain Gana secured three tablets, two of which are on deposit in the national museum at Santiago de Chili and the third was sent to France, but does not appear to have reached its destination. Paper impressions and casts were taken from the Chilian tablets for the various museums of Europe. Those sent to the English Ethnological Society created some interest after a time, but others sent to Berlin were regarded as stamps for marking native cloth (Mittheilungen, July, 1871). Seven of these tablets are now in the possession of Tepano Jansser, bishop of Axieri, all in excellent state of preservation.

While the *Mohican* was at Tahiti, the bishop kindly permitted us to examine these tablets and take photographs of them. These tablets were obtained from the missionaries who had been stationed on Easter Island, and they ranged in size from $5\frac{1}{2}$ inches in length by 4 inches broad, to $5\frac{1}{2}$ feet in length and 7 inches wide. Diligent search was made for specimens of these tablets during our visit to Easter Island. At first the natives denied having any, but Mr. Salmon knew of the existence of two, and these were finally purchased after a great deal of trouble and at considerable expense. The tablets obtained are in a fair state of preservation. The large one is a piece of drift-wood that from its peculiar shape is supposed to have been used as a portion of a canoe. The other is made of the toromiro wood indigenous to the island. In explanation of the disappearance of these tablets, the natives stated that the missionaries had ordered all that could be found to be burned, with a view to destroying the ancient records, and getting rid of everything that would have a tendency to attach them to their heathenism, and prevent their thorough conversion to Christianity. The loss to the science of philology by this destruction of valuable relics is too great to be estimated. The native traditions in regard to the incised tablets simply assert that Hotu-Matua, the first king, possessed the knowledge of this written language, and brought with him to the island sixty-seven tablets containing allegories, traditions, genealogical tables, and proverbs relating to the land from which he had migrated. A knowledge of the written characters was confined to the royal family, the chiefs of the six districts into which the island was divided, sons of those chiefs, and certain priests or teachers, but the people were assembled at Anckena Bay once each year to hear all of the tablets read. The feast of the tablets was regarded as their most important fête day, and not even war was allowed to interfere with it.

The combination of circumstances that caused the sudden arrest of image-making, and resulted in the abandonment of all such work on the island, never to be again revived, may have had its effect upon the art of writing. The tablets that have been found in the best stage of preservation would correspond very nearly with the age of the unfinished images in the workshops. The ability to read the characters may have continued until 1864, when the Peruvian slavers captured a large number of the inhabitants, and among those kidnapped, were all of the officials and persons in authority. After this outrage, the traditions, etc., embraced by the tablets, seem to have been repeated on particular occasions, but the value of the characters was not understood and was lost to the natives. A man called Ure Vaeiko, one of the patriarchs of the island, professes to have been under instructions in the art of hieroglyphic reading at the time of the Peruvian visit, and claims to understand most of the characters. Negotiations were opened with him for a translation of the two tablets purchased; but he declined to furnish any information, on the ground that it had been forbidden by the priests. Presents of money and

Obverse of Easter Island Tablet, "Apai."
(Original in possession of Bishop of Axieri.)

REVERSE OF EASTER ISLAND TABLET, "APAI."
(Original in possession of Bishop of Axieri.)

valuables were sent him from time to time, but he invariably replied to all overtures that he was now old and feeble and had but a short time to live, and declined most positively to ruin his chances for salvation by doing what his Christian instructors had forbidden. Finally the old fellow, to avoid temptation, took to the hills with the determination to remain in hiding until after the departure of the *Mohican*. It was a matter of the utmost importance that the subject should be thoroughly investigated before leaving the island, and unscrupulous strategy was the only resource after fair means had failed. Just before sundown one evening, shortly before the day appointed for our sailing, heavy clouds rolled up from the southwest and indications pointed to bad weather. In a heavy down-pour of rain we crossed the island from Vinapu to Mateveri with Mr. Salmon, and found, as had been expected, that old Ure Vaeiko had sought the shelter of his own home on this rough night. He was asleep when we entered and took charge of the establishment. When he found escape impossible he became sullen, and refused to look at or touch a tablet. As a compromise it was proposed that he should relate some of the ancient traditions. This was readily acceded to, because the opportunity of relating the legends to an interested audience did not often occur, and the positive pleasure to be derived from such an occasion could not be neglected. During the recital certain stimulants that had been provided for such an emergency were produced, and though not pressed upon our ancient friend, were kept prominently before him until, as the night grew old and the narrator weary, he was included as the "cup that cheers" made its occasional rounds. A judicious indulgence in present comforts dispelled all fears in regard to the future state, and at an auspicious moment the photographs of the tablets owned by the bishop were produced for inspection. Old Ure Vaeiko had never seen a photograph before, and was surprised to find how faithfully they reproduced the tablets which he had known in his young days. A tablet would have met with opposition, but no objection could be urged against a photograph, especially something possessed by the good bishop, whom he had been instructed to reverence. The photographs were recognized immediately, and the appropriate legend related with fluency and without hesitation from beginning to end. The story of all the tablets of which we had a knowledge was finally obtained, the words of the native being written down by Mr. Salmon as they were uttered, and afterwards translated into English.

A casual glance at the Easter Island tablets is sufficient to note the fact that they differ materially from other kyriologic writings. The pictorial symbols are engraved in regular lines on depressed channels, separated by slight ridges intended to protect the hieroglyphics from injury by rubbing. In some cases the characters are smaller, and the tablets contain a greater number of lines, but in all cases the hieroglyphics are incised and cover both sides as well as the beveled edges and hollows of the board upon which they are engraved. The symbols on each line are alternately reversed; those on the first stand upright, and those on the next line are upside down, and so on by regular alternation.

This unique plan makes it necessary for the reader to turn the tablet and change its position at the end of every line; by this means the characters will be found to follow in regular procession. The reading should commence at the lower left-hand corner, on the particular side that will bring the figures erect, and followed as the characters face in the procession, turning the tablet at the end of each line, as indicated. Arriving at the top of the first face, the reading is continued over the edge to the nearest line, at the top of the other side, and the descent continues in the same manner until the end is reached. The Bonstrophedon method is supposed to have been adopted in order to avoid the possibility of missing a line of hieroglyphics.

Ure Vaeiko's fluent interpretation of the tablet was not interrupted, though it became evident that he was not actually reading the characters. It was noticed that the shifting of position did not accord with the number of symbols on the lines, and afterwards when the photograph of another tablet was substituted, the same story was continued without the change being discovered. The old fellow was quite discomposed when charged with fraud at the close of an all-night session, and at first maintained that the characters were all understood, but he could not give the signification of hieroglyphics copied indiscriminately from tablets already marked. He explained at great length that the actual value and significance of the symbols had been forgotten, but the tablets were recognized by unmistakable features and the interpretation of them was beyond question; just as a person might recognize a book in a foreign language and be perfectly sure of the contents without being able to actually read it.

Beyond doubt certain legends are ascribed to particular tablets, all of which are named, and a reference to those names will recall the appropriate story from those who do not profess to understand the hieroglyphics. An old man called Kaitae, who claims relationship to the last king, Maurata, afterwards recognized several of the tablets from the photographs and related the same story exactly as that given previously by Ure Vaeiko.

The writing is composed of pictorial symbols carrying their signification in the image they represent. The execution would be a creditable production with the assistance of the best etching tools, and is a truly wonderful result of patience and industry to be accomplished by means of obsidian points. The minute size of the hieroglyphics made it impossible to convey anything more than the general appearance of the objects delineated, but the figures may be recognized by their form in the outline drawing after the manner of some of the Egyptian hieroglyphics. The study of the tablets is chiefly difficult on account of the way in which actual objects are conventionally treated, and in order to preserve symmetry and effect, men, canoes, fish, etc., are represented of the same size throughout the lines.

A careful study of the hieroglyphics of Easter Island is being made with the hope that valuable information may be obtained in regard to the early history and origin of the people. Results of an extremely interesting nature are barely outlined at present and not in shape to be presented herewith. It is not considered expedient to attempt an explanation of the symbols until the subject can be treated exhaustively. As an example of the ideographic character of the signs, the tablet containing the genealogical tables shows a frequent repetition of the symbol of the great spirit Meke-Meke in connection with that of the female vulva. The signification is the birth of a person. The position of the figures shows whether the child was the result of marriage, or intrigue, and the following figures indicate the date of the birth, the seasons and the approximate time. An important feature, in connection with the tablets, is the fact that forms have been discovered which have no types on Easter Island, and which may lead to an identification of the locality from whence the first settlers migrated. The hieroglyphics include, besides the representation of actual objects, figures used by the chiefs, and each clan had its distinctive mark. Samples are given in different treaties made with the islanders of the sign-manual of some of the chiefs. (See. Plates XXXVI-XLIX.)

TRANSLATION OF EASTER ISLAND TABLETS.

APAI.

(Plates XXXVI and XXXVII.)

Timo te kakaha piki apai te roria aruki e tangata Mohonâkuta mohonga matangi eiri apai ia ra Techo i te ika mahoi rua matangi apai tirori mahoi rua matangi tahoi te tha tahoi hakavirri ia tapui rurenga tahri te ika tahoi te ata e tau ira tau na mimi hara rau kina ata rangi no no tupa kan k maka reva atea e tau ira matuku hara atarungi no no tapairu renga ava ki hoato.

Houa kata-kata hura matini rau hanga tamaru kia tun ama tavake toto tunmakeuka tantan mea te kura. Ki hi honga te kura e aku tapaini kari mao aku hoa-hoa tae kote kura mata ki rei aaku tapa iru nei kairi mai aku hora-hora tae kote kura.

Mata ki rei mata ku haka iri marai matairi maru matai maru ka irira tapui rei tapui ranga muku kiri mai aku hoa-hoa tae kote kura. Mata. ki rei mata ku haka iri maru matai marn matai rara ku uira tapni rei tapui rei tapu ranga muku kairi mai aku hora-hora kapainga mai. E. tangaroa te mare kura hapai e haka ihi mo topa rei kura taku tapo rei hun atu arna tae haath rangi ura rangi hara-tua oaku matua oaku ma tenga otae ahiri noa ranga ki te raugi no te mununiri a rua hiru te hetu takiri ko mumu ana kia kake mao-mao ake. Haka tau Era a Nuku te atua. Atara kahiria a uka hopua. Tun haka maua kura. Tun te ha. hei kura. Tun te tieuituiri kura. Tun te matangi e ria a mangaro.

Tun tahake oi taura te herunga taku ohu tutuhinga tanku mato kapipiri te hetun tan aranga noi ruga vake noi runga. Maruaua ha heire mana mahahine manaira taake. Te herunga taku oho te tuhinga taku mata mata ka pipiri te hetn tau avanga no iringa vake-vake. No iri uga vake rei manana hahinie E te mai ran o tun e katau, râ, ka piapiri râ e te maraioturi e kakapura e kahakpiri e kahonotake mate aa tapu onote ariiki no Manana hahine no Mananatake a niramai te rangi kai a ku ia umika uri te hainu tokotokona to rau e nui a tapu te tai nate ariiki. E. hopu a ia e tapu te tai no te tapa iru e kore kaukau â ia haharua tau kapa tau kaiugoh i te an mata heuna, mariunga te hon i te au mataheune mariunga te houga ma tau arapeka hoa mai ia keho iti hiti aura hiti apanoko hue taka baahaarua tau kape tau hai ugoto piria tamu ara te uaua na Heke i kai te hunue kura te nahoapu, pue hatataka i te an mata mo tara haieka i te peka akatau o mirunga te hounga mo tara haieka. Panga tiorei nuku horo papa tara naeaki i te pou tuu. Panga te orei nuku horo papa hoake mataue uake tahau te uauai e oho te nauai e rai te nauau nauai kino noho avaava tauake te kete ironga te niu ei ia hoa ko ni ni ei ia hoa o Rionou tona koake mâtoue uake te nauai e oho te uauai e rai te uauai nauai nauai kino nohi ava ava taua kate kete iringa te niu haamatua nauai kino katangi te moko-moko uri katangi te moko-moko tea kohao kopirieuta moko-moko uri ua moko-moko tea takaia rangi kakae hoki i te atua. Mohao haruru vai e kahihinga ma te tougakapitia rangi mokomoko uri moko moko tea kohao kopiri e atua mamairi kauaha itu atimo eae aruarua vori kahihiua mo te Tonga kahuhinga ma te Tonga nui kahinga i tongarou kapitia rangi moko moko uri moko-moko tea pruho kauaha uri korueiha Hangaroa a Timeo eae e te Raki ete roroe taua erua aaku manu.

Hakarongo noa i te reo o te moa e vai-vai mahaui ia ure roroi renga aha iho nei e te ahine ariikie ouku ika na kio i varimariaria hopue hara koe e rara a eau i te taura hiku raverave a hiro kai te teri hepo e tao koe hoki napa te ingoa taua ika ko mumu marauga ugaiatu ko pephu ko pepetangi. ko pepetangi taravi tavi. ko pepetangi tava taravi tava e hakanui koe ki te ehu koe ki te kapua. Tun hitu hare ka more koe kapai tue.

ENGLISH TRANSLATION OF APAI TRADITION.

Mohouakuta, the chief of a powerful clan, when about to make war to revenge the death of one of his relatives, who had been killed by treachery, summoned Timo, the builder of fowl-houses, and ordered him to construct on the windward side of the house of Tecbo, the fisherman, a fowl-house of one hundred cresent-shaped stakes. It was ordered that of the fowls captured in the war those with long tail-feathers, and the white ones, should be reserved and sent to this house for safe-keeping.

The warriors of the clan assembled promptly at the council-fire with their faces brilliantly painted and wearing their distinctive shell necklaces.

The solemn ceremonies, attendant upon the declaration of war, were performed by the assembled braves, in accordance with the ancient customs handed down by their forefathers. Obeisance was first made to the sky, each warrior repeating the prayer, "May we be killed in battle if we neglect to worship the Great Spirit." The ceremonies concluded with obeisance to the god of feathers, each warrior wearing the feather-hat of his clan—Era Nuku, the god of feathers, whose costume consists of feathers for the head, feathers for the neck, and feathers to be waved by the wind. He who brings good luck when feathers are worn that are tied by a string of hair. He who protects the yams and potato plantations when feathers are tied upon a stick, and placed close together between the hills. He who keeps off the evil spirit when feathers are planted over the burial-places.

The god of feathers, whose wife is Manana. Manana Take came from the skies. She once visited the land in the shape of a fish, which was captured and given to the king on account of its size and beauty. Recognizing the divine nature of the fish, the king was thereafter debarred from swimming in the sea.

(The next hieroglyphics on the tablet are supposed to have been written in some ancient language, the key to which has long ago been lost. After this unknown section the translation is continued as follows):

When the island was first created and became known to our forefathers, the land was crossed with roads beautifully paved with flat stones. The stones were laid close together so artistically that no rough edges were exposed. Coffee-trees were growing close together along the borders of the road, that met overhead, and the branches were laced together like muscles. Heke was the builder of these roads, and it was he, who sat in the place of honor in the middle where the roads branched away in every direction. These roads were cunningly contrived to represent the plan of the web of the gray and black-pointed spider, and no man could discover the beginning or the end thereof.

(Here again are some sections of the tablet written in the characters that are not understood, after which the following translation is made:)

In that happy land, that beautiful land where Romaha formerly lived with his beloved Hangaroa, and where Turaki used to listen to the voice of the fowl, and feed them with watery food. In that beautiful land that was governed by gods from heaven, and who lived in the water when it was cold. Where the black and white-pointed spider would have mounted to heaven, but was prevented by the bitterness of the cold.

Where is our ancient queen? It is known that she was transformed into a fish that was finally caught in the still waters. A fish that had to be tied by the rope of Heros to be captured. Away, away, if you can not name the fish. That lovely fish with the short gills that was brought for food to our Great King, and was laid upon a dish that rocked this way and that. The same that afterwards formed the corner of the stone walk that led to the house of the Great Chief.

TRANSLATION OF THE EASTER ISLAND TABLETS.

ATUA MATARIRI.

(Plates XXXVIII and XXXIX.)

Atua Matariri; Ki ai Kiroto, Kia Taporo, Kapu te Poporo.
Ahimahima Marao; Ki ai Kiroto, Takihi Tupufema, Kapu te Kibikebi.
Aoevai; Ki ai Kiroto, Kava Kohe Koe Kapu te Koe.
Matua anua; Ki ai Kiroto, Kappipiri Haitau, Kapu te Miro.
Augiugieai; Ki ai Kiroto, Kia Humutoti, Kapu te Maluta.
Hiti; Ki ai Kiroto, Kia Heta Kapu te Ti.
Atura; Ki ai Kiroto, Katei, Kapu te Monku Uta.
Ahan; Ki ai Kiroto, Vava, Kapu te Tureme.
Ahekai; Ki ai Kiroto, Hepeue, Kapu te Mataa.
Viri Koue; Ki ai Kiroto, Ariugarehe Uruharero, Kapu te Runa.
Atua Metua; Ki ai Kiroto, Kariritunarai, Kapu te Niu.
Atua Metua; Ki ai Kiroto, Kite Vuhi o Atua, Kapu te Toromiro.
Atua Metua; Ki ai Kiroto, Tapuhavaoatua, Kapu te Moana.
A Heuru; Ki ai Kiroto, Hetomu, Kapu te Marikuru.
A Taveke; Ki ai Kiroto, Pouhutubututerevaimangaro, Kapu te Veke.
A Hahamea; Ki ai Kiroto, Hohio Kapu te Takure.
Aukia Ki ai Kiroto; Moremanga, Kapu te Ngarava.
Avia Moko; Ki ai Kiroto, Viatea, Kapu te Kena.
Tereheue; Ki ai Kiroto, Viaraupa, Kapu te Kaupa.
A Heroe; Ki ai Kiroto, Uuhipura, Mapu te Ro.
Tahatoi; Ki ai Kiroto, Kateapiairiroro, Kapu te To.
Irapupue; Ki ai Kiroto, Irakaka, Kapu te Pia.
Mangeougeo; Ki ai Kiroto, Herakiraki Kapu te Kape.
A Hen; Ki ai Kiroto Pana Kapu te Hue.
Heima; Ki ai Kiroto Kairui Kairui-Hakamarui Kapu te Raa.
Huruau; Ki ai Kiroto Hiuaoio Kapu te Moa.
A Hikua: Ki ai Kiroto Hinaoioi Kapu te Uruara.
Tingahae: Ki ai Kiroto Parararahikutea Kapu te Niuki.
A Hikue: Ki ai Kiroto Hiuaoioi Kapu te Tabraha.

OBVERSE OF EASTER ISLAND WOODEN TABLET, "A TUA MATARIRI."

(Cat. No. 129773, U. S. N. M. Easter Island. Collected and deposited by Paymaster W. J. Thomson, U. S. N.)

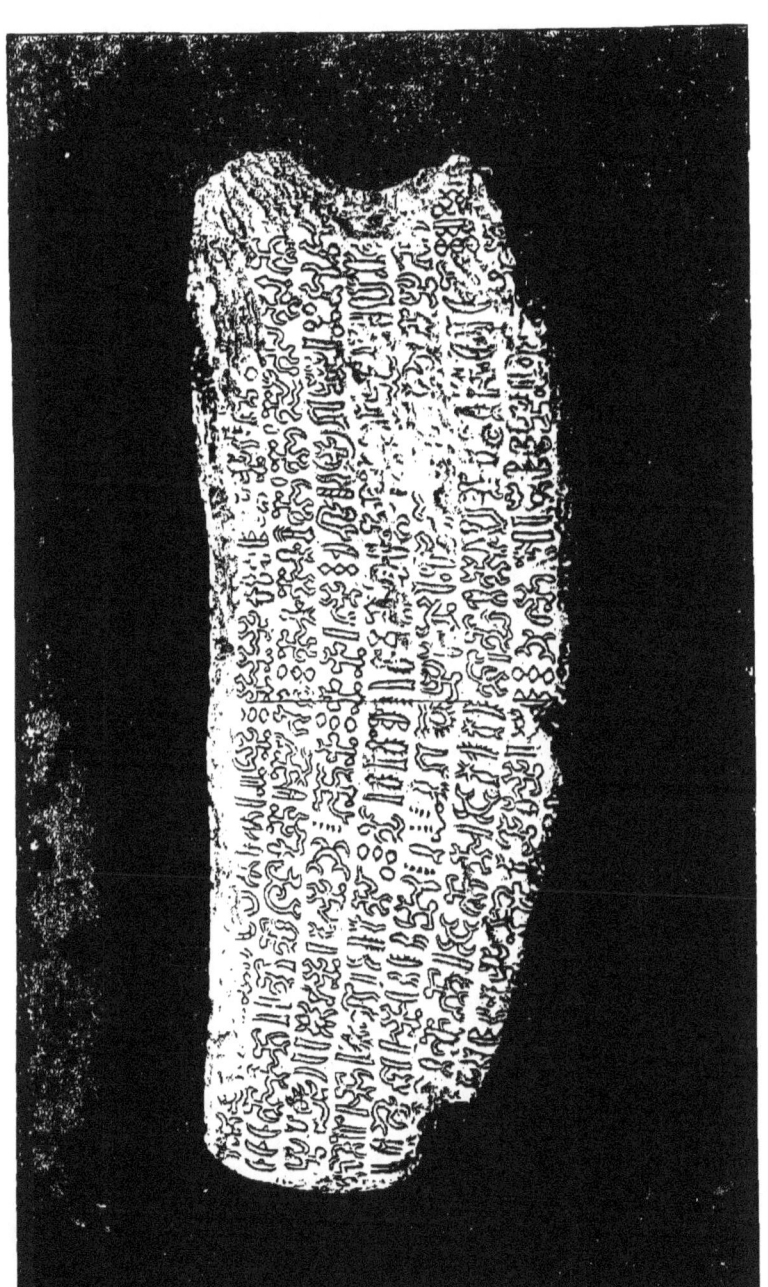

REVERSE OF EASTER ISLAND WOODEN TABLET, "ATUA MATARIRI."
(Cat. No. 129773, U. S. N. M. Easter Island. Collected and deposited by Paymaster W. J. Thomson, U. S. N.)

Tikitehatu: Ki ai Kiroto Hilobihokiteturu Kapu te Paroko.
Tikitehatu: Ki ai Kiroto Hinapopoia Kapu te Hiuakuhara.
Tikitehatu: Ki ai Kiroto Maea Kapu te Heraherakitomea.
Tikitehatu: Ki ai Kiroto Ruruatikitehatu Kapu te Teririkatea.
Atimoterae: mea a mura i biki te alu mo tunu o te ita. mo haugai it te ariiki.
Takoua: Ki ai Kiroto Tukouo, Kapu te Poopoo.
E. Toto te Efi no Kino no naroko no ngaoreno no nga tokutoko ruapapa.
Epuoko te unika no tupa iti no tupa uui.
Uku Ki ai Kiroto, Karori Kapu te Ngaatu.
Kuhikia Ki ai Kiroto Taurari Kapu to Ngaatu.
Kuhikia Ki ai Kiroto Ruperoa Kapu to Turi.
Taaria Ki ai Kiroto Taaria, Kapu te Taueehu.
Hainge Ki ai Kiroto hatukuti, Kapu te Evea.
Pauaroroko Ki ai Kiroto Hakukuti, Kapu te Taerongoveteve.
Hiuitirerire Ki ai Kiroto Kanohotatataporo Kapu te Roporo.
Numia a Taugaire Turuhirohero te toto o te o korare.
Kamau te Korare taratara te Korare.
Turuki te Ua Maanau Manavai roa.
Kauuuku raituahea anakihorou eaa e to e tua tanu to tana moko eaha Uaugai e to e ufi e Kumara.

ENGLISH TRANSLATION OF THE ABOVE TABLET.

EASTER ISLAND TRADITION.

The origin of inanimate things is believed to be the result of the marriage of certain gods and goddesses in accordance with the following table.

God Atua Matariri and goddess Taporo produced thistle.
God Ahimahima Marao and goddess Takihi Tupufema produced rocks.
God Aocvai and goddess Kava Kohekoe produced medicine.
God Matua anua and goddess Kappipiri Aaitau produced the Miro tree.
God Angingieai and goddess Kia Humutoti produced the paper-mulberry tree.
God Hiti and goddess Kia heta produced the tea plant.
God Atura and goddess Katei produced bunch grass.
God Ahen and goddess Vaua produced fine grass.
God Agekai and goddess Hepene produced obsidian.
God Viri Kone and goddess Ariugarehe Uruharero produced the morning-glory plant.

God Atua Metua and goddess Kariritunaria produced cocoanuts.
God Atua Metua and goddess Ki te Vuhi o Atua produced the toromiro tree.
God Atua Metua and goddess Tapuhavaoatua produced Hibiscus.
God A Heuru and goddess Hetomu produced the blue leaf plant.
God A Taveke and goddess Pouhutuhututereraimangaro, produced the white ash.
God A Hahamea and goddess Hohio produced flies.
God Ankia and goddess Moremanuga produced roaches.
God A Via Moko and goddess Viatea produced boobies.
God Tereheue and goddess Viaranpa produced leaves.
God A Heroe and goddess Unhipura produced ants.
God Tahatoi and goddess Kateapiairiroro produced sugar-cane.
God Irapupue and goddess Irakaka produced arrowroot.
God Mangeongeo and goddess Herakiraki produced yams.
God Ahen and goddess Pana produced calabash.
God Heima and goddess Kairui-hakamarui produced stars.
God Huruan and goddess Hiuaoioi produced fowls.
God A Hikua and goddess Hiuaoioi produced vermilion.
God Tiugahae and goddess Pararahikutea produced sharks.
God A Hikue and goddess Hiuaoioi produced porpoise.
God Tikitehatu and goddess Hihohihokiteturu produced rock-fish.
God Tikitehatu and goddess Hiuapopoia produced life.
God Tikitehatu and goddess Maea produced luck.
God Tikitehatu and goddess Ruruatikitehatu produced man.
Atimoterae created brook-fish and established them as the chosen food of the gods.
God Takoua and goddess Tukouo produced milk-thistle.
E Toto discovered the sweet taste of the yam and made it the principal food of the people.
Epnoko created the delicious banana food for the kings.
God Uku and goddess Karori produced bullrushes.
God Kuhikia and goddess Taurari produced small birds.
God Kuhikia and goddess Ruperoa produced sea-gulls.
God Taaria and goddess Taaria produced white gulls.
God Haluge and goddess Hatukuti produced wind.
God Pauaroroko and goddess Hakukuti produced pain.
God Hiuitirerire and goddess Kanohotatataporo produced creeping vines.
Numia a Tangaire Turuhirohero was the founder of all things unpleasant and bad smells.
Turuki was the first builder of rock fences and barriers.
Kuanuku created death by drowning, death in warfare, death by accident, and death by disease.

TE PITO TE HENUA, OR EASTER ISLAND. 523

TRANSLATION OF EASTER ISLAND TABLETS.

EAHA TO RAN ARIIKI KETE.

(Plates XL and XLI.)

1. Eaha to ran ariiki kete mahua i uta nei?
   E tupu tomo a mata mea e rangi ran e tuatea to ran ariiki kete mahua i uta nei.
   Ane rato mani rata karata te tuatea, karata te rangi ran karata te tupuna.
2. Eaha to ran ariiki kete mahua i uta nei?
   E ura e poopoo e koiro e nohoe e to ran ariiki kete mahua i uta nei.
   Ane rato mani rata karata te ura ki kara te poopoo e nehe e riku e kava-kava atu.
3. Eaha to ran ariiki kete mahua i uta nei?
   E nehe e riku e kava atua to ran ariiki kete mahua i uta nei.
   Ane rato mani rata karata te nehe karata riku karata rain kava atua.
4. Eaha to ran ariiki kete mahua i uta nei?
   E a hao nei e kahi e atu e ature.
   Ane rato mani rata karata te kahi kaharta ahi rarata te ature ane rato.
5. Eaha to ran ariiki kete mahua i uta nei?
   E ufi e tra e kumaro to ran ariiki mahua i uta nei.
   Ane rato karata te ufi kumara toa e mahna i uta nei, ane rato maru.
6. Eaha to ran ariiki kete mahua i uta nei?
   E honu e kea e pane te ran ariiki kete mahua i nta nei.
   Ane rato karata te honu te kea te pane.
7. Eaha to ran ariiki kete mahua i uta nei?
   E hetu e range e han e na e raa e mahua te ran ariiki kete mahua i irunga nei.
   Ane rato karata te rangi e hon e na e raa e mahua.
8. Eaha te ran ariiki kete mahua i uta nei?
   E annga nei karata te hehun rangi han na raa mahua.
   Ane rato karata te hehun rangi han na raa mahua.
9. Eaha to ran ariiki kete mahua i uta nei?
   E ariiki e tapairu to ran ariiki kete i mahua i mua nei.
   Ane rato karata to ariiki te tapairu.
10. Eaha to ran ariiki kete mahua i uta nei?
    E oi e potupotu e ugarara e hata to ran ariiki kete mahua i uta nei.
    Ane rato karata main rata e oi e potupotu e ugarara e hata to ran ariiki kete mahua i uta uei.

ENGLISH TRANSLATION OF TABLET.

EASTER ISLAND ANTHEM.

What power has the Great King on the land?
He has power to make the plants grow and to change the sky to different colors.
All hail the power of the Great King who makes us lenient to the

young plants, to admire the skies of different colors, and to behold the clouds that rise.

What power has the Great King on the land?

He has the power to create the lobsters, white-bait, eels, ape-fish, and everything in the sea.

All hail the power of the Great King who gives us the knowledge of how to catch the lobsters, white-bait, eels, ape-fish, and all marine animals.

What power has the Great King on the land?

He has the power to produce the ferns, creeping plants, grass, bushes, and all vegetation.

All hail the power of the Great King who has taught us to love the ferns, creeping plants, and all green things.

What power has the Great King over the sea?

He has the power to create the mighty fish that swim in the deep water.

All hail the power of the Great King who has given us the strength and skill to catch the fish of the mighty deep.

What power has the Great King on the land?

He has the power to produce the yams, potatoes, and sugar-cane.

All hail the power of the Great King who enables us to use as food yams, potatoes, and sugar-cane.

What power has the Great King on the land?

He has the power to clothe the turtles in hard shell, the fish with scales, and protects every living thing.

All hail the power of the Great King who enables us to overcome the defense of the turtles, fish, and all reptiles.

What power has the Great King in the universe?

He has the power to create the stars, the clouds, the dew, the rain, the sun, and the moon.

All hail the power of the Great King who enables us to appreciate the blessings of the bright stars, the lowering clouds, the gentle dew, the falling rain, and the light of the sun and moon.

What power has the Great King upon the land?

He has the power to populate the earth, to create both kings and subjects.

All hail the power of the Great King who has created the human beings, given authority to kings, and created loyal subjects.

What power has the Great King upon the land?

He has the power to create maggots, flies, worms, fleas, and all creeping and flying insects.

All hail the power of the Great King who enables us to withstand the attacks of the maggots, flies, worms, fleas, and all manner of insects.

What power has the Great King?

All hail the unlimited power of the Great King.

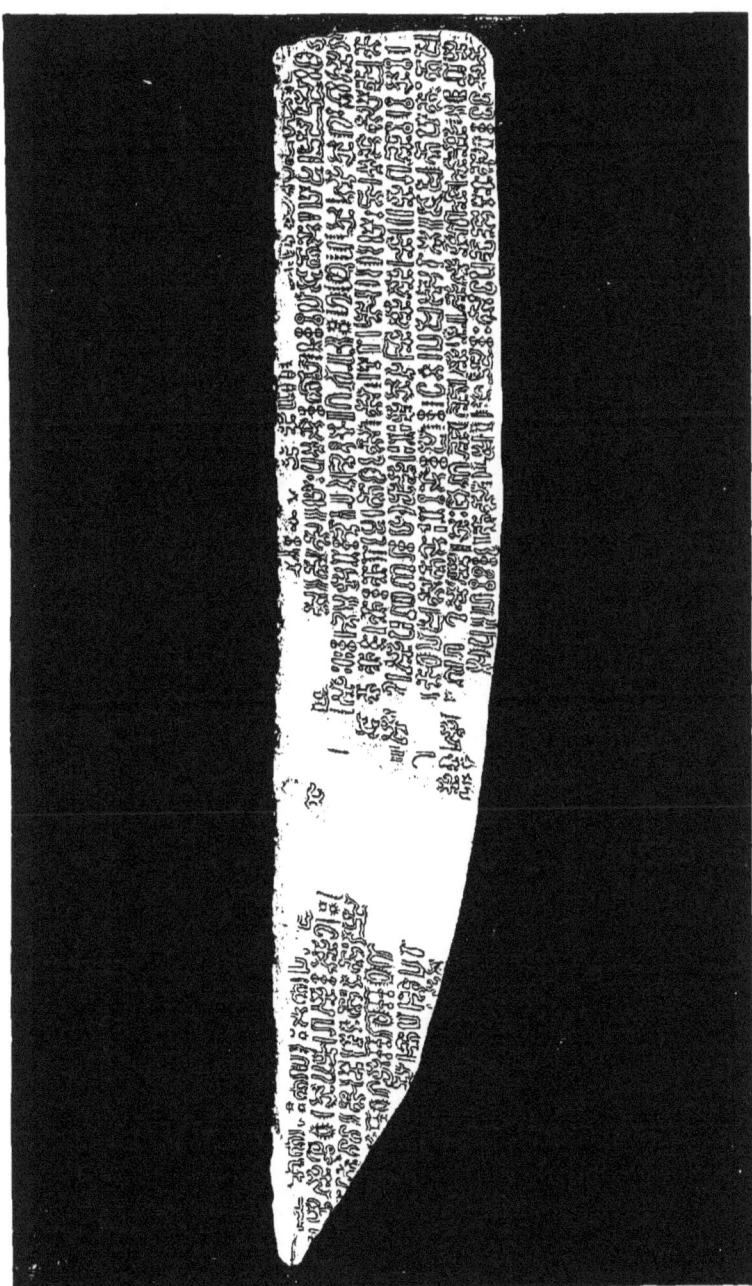

OBVERSE OF EASTER ISLAND WOODEN TABLET, "EAHA TO RAN ARIIKI KETE."

(Cat. No. 129774, U. S. N. M. Easter Island. Collected and deposited by Paymaster W. J. Thomson, U. S. N.)

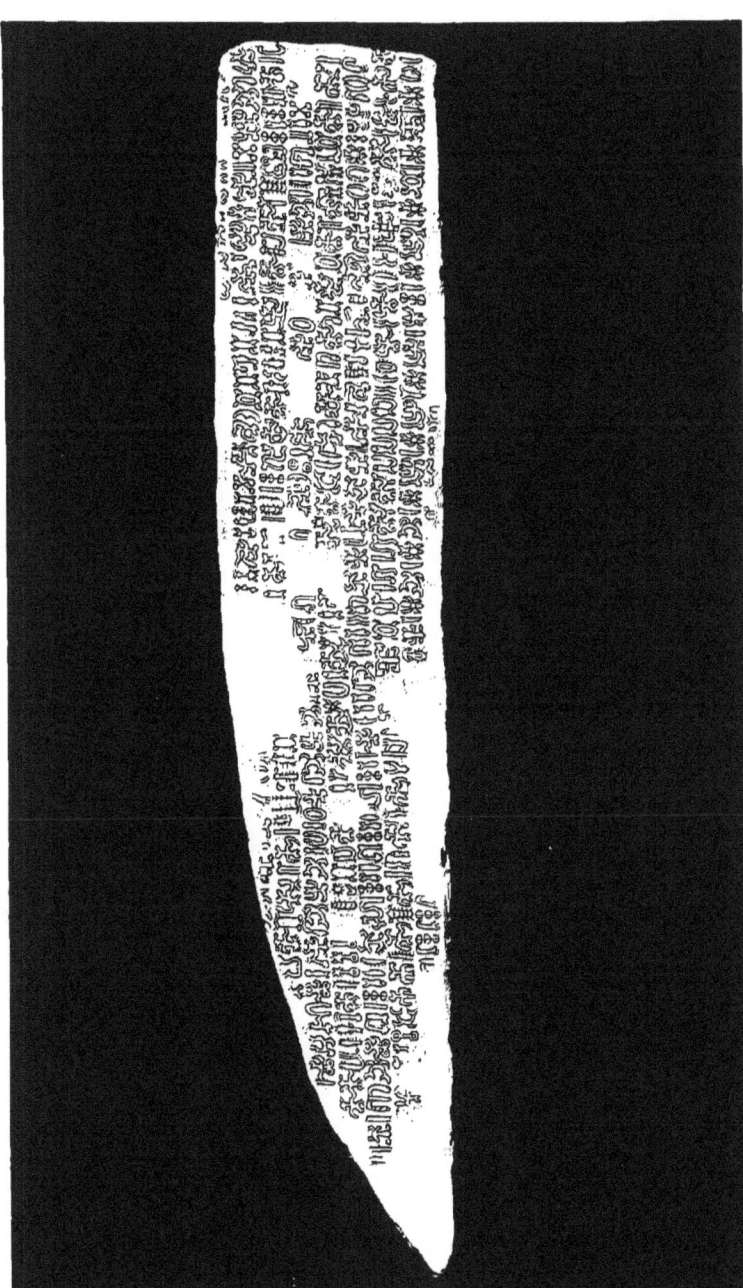

Reverse of Easter Island wooden Tablet. "Eaha to ran ariiki kete."
(Cat. No. 129774, U. S. N. M. Easter Island. Collected and deposited by Paymaster W. J. Thomson, U. S. N.)

TE PITO TE HENUA, OR EASTER ISLAND. 525

TRANSLATION OF EASTER ISLAND TABLETS.

FATHER MOURNING THE LOSS OF HIS CHILD.

(Plates XLII and XLIII.)

Ka ihi niga — te ki ati —
  Auwe te poki, e —
Ite maki tana — Rii te hiva iua.
Ka ihi niga — mai.

2.

Ka ihi niga — te ki ati —
  Auwe te poki, e —
Ite maki tana — Honiti ina.
Ka ihi uiga — moa mai.

3.

Ha imn, — poki — e — ;
  Ta auwe rai — e;
Viviri rai, ioage — o ;
  I — ruga — i ;
  Te papare hinna
Viviri rai — iunge — o !

4.

Haki — e !
Avahinua — ki tagn atu.
  Auwe poki — e !
Ava rai —
Ava mata — Ina hiva
  Auwe poki — o !
Ite renia o parapa moui
  Auwe poki — e !

This is an old song, supposed to have descended from the time the first inhabitants arrived on the island. The father is believed to mourn for his child left in that eastern land, from which tradition states the people migrated.

ENGLISH TRANSLATION.

The sail of my daughter,
  Never broken by the force of foreign clans!
The sail of my daughter,
  Unbroken by the conspiracy of Honiti!
Ever victorious in all her fights
  She could not be enticed to drink poison waters
In the cup of obsidian glass.
  Can my sorrow ever be appeased
While we are divided by the mighty seas?
  Oh my daughter, oh my daughter!
It is a vast and watery road
  Over which I look toward the horizon,
My daughter, oh my daughter!
  I'll swim over the deep to meet you,
My daughter, oh my daughter!

TRANSLATION OF EASTER ISLAND TABLET.

"*Ate-a-renga-hokan iti poheraa.*"

LOVE SONG.

(Plates XLIV and XLV.)

Ka tagi, Renga-a-manu — hakaopa;
Chiu ruuarame a ita ructua.
Ka ketu te nairo bihi — O te hoa!
Eaha ton tiena — e te hoa — e!

Ita haga ta poapatu — O te hoa!
Kahii te riva foraui — O te hoa — e!
Auwe ka tagi ati — u — a — iti iti.
Eha ton tieua — e ta hoa — e.

Ta hi tiena ita have.
Horoa ita have.
Horoa moni e fahiti;
Ita ori miro;
Aua piri atu;
Ana piri atu;
Ana taga atu.

ENGLISH TRANSLATION.

NATIVE LOVE SONG,

Who is sorrowing? It is Renga-a-manu Hakopa!
A red branch descended from her father.
Open thine eyelids, my true love.
Where is your brother, my love?
At the feast in the Bay of Salutation
We will meet under the feathers of your clan.
She has long been yearning after you.
Send your brother as a mediator of love between us,
Your brother who is now at the house of my father.
O, where is the messenger of love between us?
When the feast of drift-wood is commemorated
There we will meet in loving embrace.

TRADITION IN REGARD TO THE ORIGIN OF THE ISLANDERS.

The island was discovered by King Hotu-Matua, who came from the land in the direction of the rising sun, with two large double canoes and three hundred chosen followers. They brought with them potatoes, yams, bananas, tobacco, sugar-cane, and the seeds of various plants, including the paper mulberry and the toromiro trees. The first landing was made on the islet of Motu Nui, on the north coast, and there the first food was cooked that had been tasted for one hundred and twenty days. The next day the queen started in one of the canoes to explore the coast to the northwest, while the other canoe, in charge of the king, rounded the island to the southeast. At Anekena Bay the

OBVERSE OF WOODEN TABLET FROM EASTER ISLAND. "KA IHI UIGA."
(From photographs presented by George Davidson to the California Academy of Sciences.)

REVERSE OF WOODEN TABLET FROM EASTER ISLAND. "KA IHI UIGA."
(From photographs presented by George Davidson to the California Academy of Sciences.)

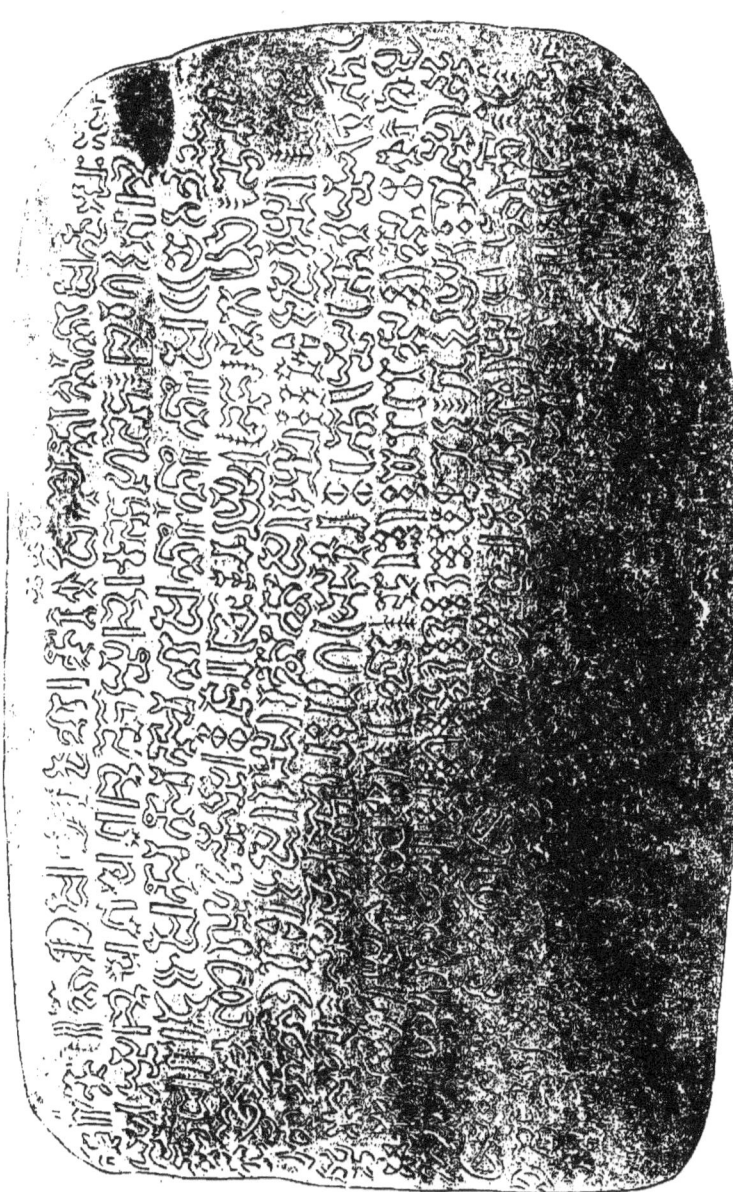

Obverse of Wooden Tablet from Easter Island. "Ate-a-renga-hokan iti Poheraa."
(Original in possession of Bishop of Axieri. From photograph by Paymaster W. J. Thomson, U. S. N.)

PLATE XLV.

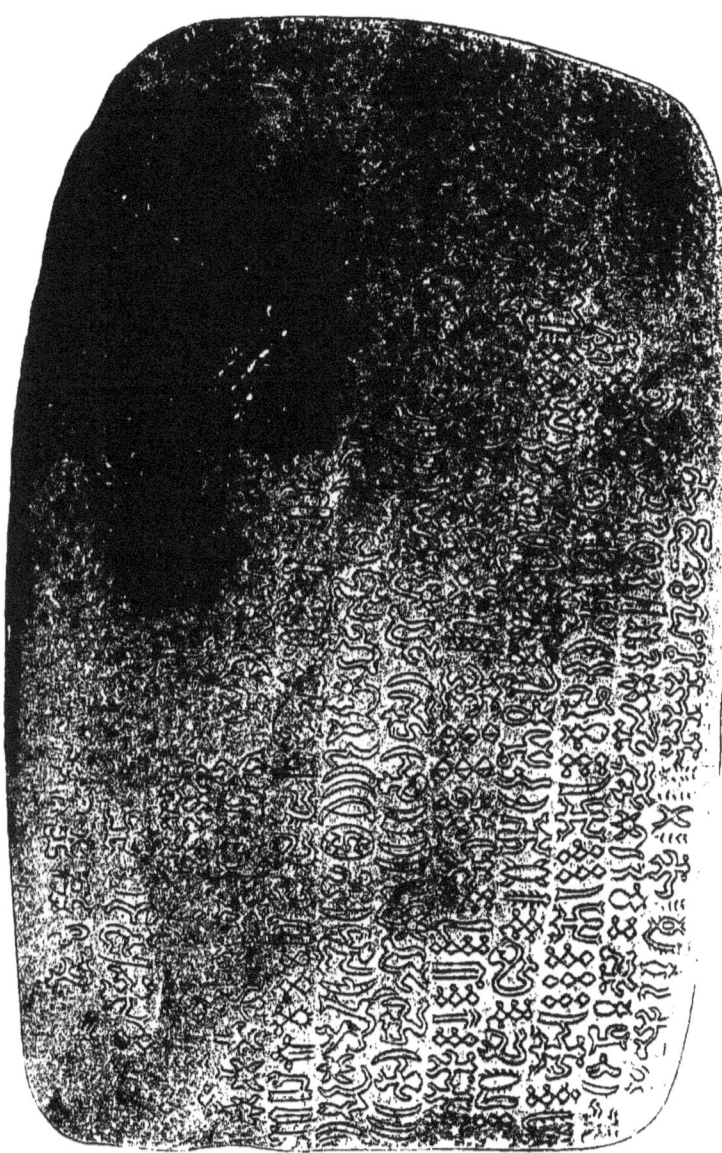

REVERSE OF WOODEN TABLET FROM EASTER ISLAND. "ATE-A-RENGA-HOKAN ITI POHERAA."
(Original in possession of Bishop of Axieri. From photograph by Paymaster W. J. Thomson, U. S. N.)

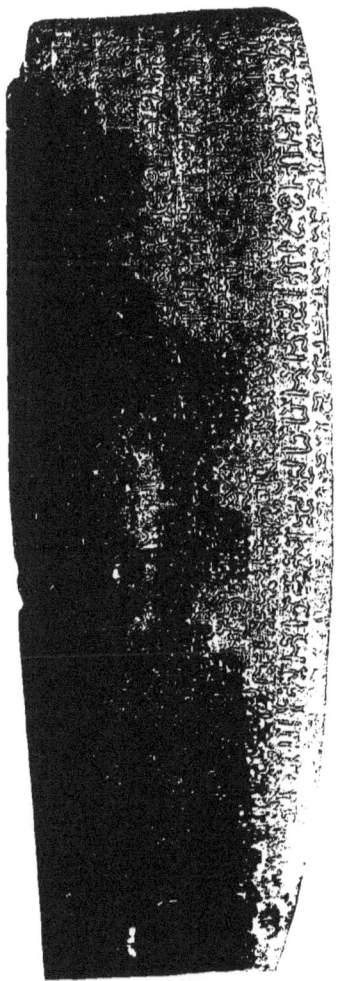

OBVERSE AND REVERSE OF EASTER ISLAND TABLET.
(From a cast lent by Parke, Davis & Co.)

Reverse of Easter Island Tablet, obtained by the Chilian corvette "O'Higgins."
(Original in Santiago Museum, Chili.)

OBVERSE OF EASTER ISLAND TABLET, OBTAINED BY THE CHILIAN CORVETTE "O'HIGGINS."
(Original in Santiago Museum, Chili.)

PLATE XLIX.

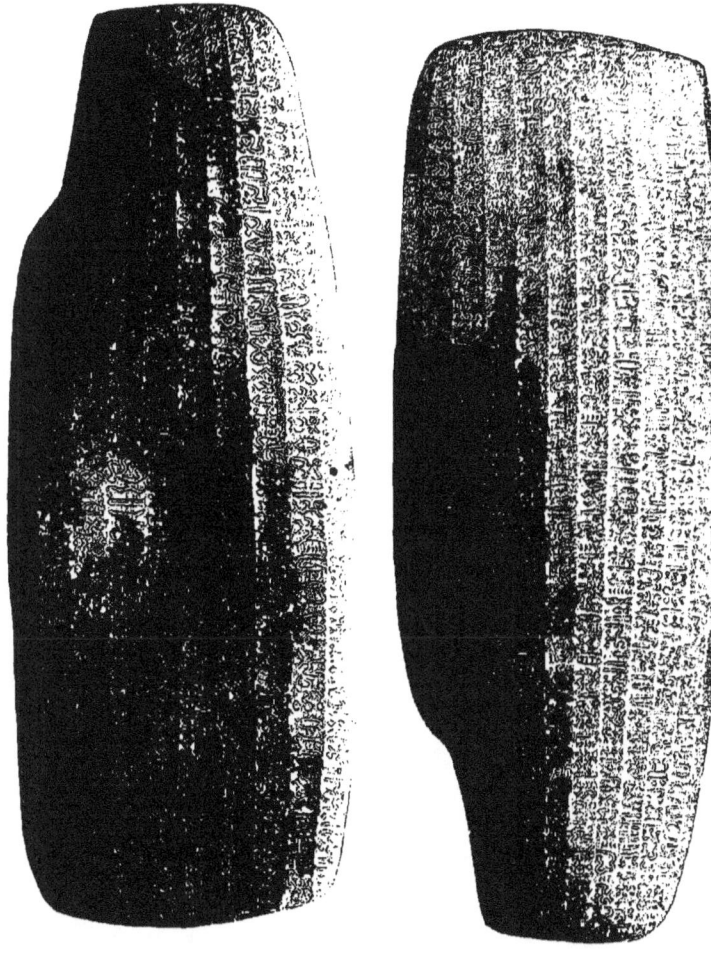

OBVERSE AND REVERSE OF EASTER ISLAND TABLET, OBTAINED BY THE CHILIAN CORVETTE "O'HIGGINS."
(Original in Santiago Museum, Chili.)

two canoes met and, attracted by the smooth sand-beach, Hotu-Matua landed and named the island "Te-pito te-henua" or "the navel of the deep." The queen landed, and immediately afterwards, gave birth to a boy, who was named Tuumae-Keke. The landing place was named Anekena in honor of the month of August, in which the island was discovered. All the plants landed from the canoes were appropriated for seed, and the people immediately began the cultivation of the ground. For the first three months they subsisted entirely upon fish, turtle, and the nuts of a creeping-plant found growing along the ground, which was named "moki-oo-ne." After the lapse of a number of unrecorded years, during which the island had been made to produce an abundance of food, and the people had increased and multiplied in numbers, Hotu-Matua at an advanced age was stricken with a mortal illness. Before his end drew near, the chief men were summoned to meet in council. The king nominated his eldest son as his successor (Tuumae-Heke), and it was ordained that the descent of the kings should always be through the eldest son. This important matter having been settled, the island was divided up into districts and portioned out to the children of the king as follows: To Tuumae-Heke, the eldest, were given the royal establishment and lands extending from Anekena to the northwest as far as Mounga Tea-tea. To Meru, the second son, were given the lands between Anekena and Hanga-roa. To Marama, the third son, were given the lands between Akahanga and Vinapu. The land lying to the northward and westward of Mounga Tea-tea was the portion of the fourth son, Raa, and was called Hanga-Toe. To the fifth son, Korona-rouga, were allotted the lands between Anekena and the crater of Rana-Roraku. To the sixth and the last son were given the lands on the east side of the island. His name was Hotu-iti.

The tradition here goes back before the advent of the people on the island, and states that Hotu-Matua and his followers came from a group of islands lying towards the rising sun, and the name of the land was Marae-toe-hau, the literal meaning of which is "the burial place." In this land, the climate was so intensely hot that the people sometimes died from the effects of the heat, and at certain seasons plants and growing things were scorched and shriveled up by the burning sun.

The circumstances that led to the migration are related as follows: Hotu-Matua succeeded his father, who was a powerful chief, but his reign in the land of his birth, owing to a combination of circumstances over which he had no control, was limited to a very few years. His brother, Machaa, fell in love with a maiden famed for her beauty and grace, but a rival appeared upon the scene in the person of Oroi, the powerful chief of a neighboring clan. After the manner of the sex in all ages and climes, this dusky beauty trifled with the affections of her suitors and proved fickle-minded. When pressed to make a choice between the two, she announced that she would marry Oroi, provided he would prove his love by making a pilgrimage around the island,

and it was specified that he should walk continually without stopping to eat, or to rest by day or night, until the tour of the island was completed. Retainers were selected to carry food to be eaten on the route, and Oroi started upon his journey, accompanied for the first few miles by his affianced bride, who promised upon parting, to permit her thoughts to dwell upon nothing but him until his return. The inconstant female eloped with her other lover, Machaa, on the same evening. Oroi did not hear this news until he had arrived at the farther end of the island; then he returned directly to his home, where he prepared a great feast to which he summoned all the warriors of his clan. The indignity that had been put upon him was related, and all present registered a vow that they would never rest until Hotu-Matua and his entire family had been put to death.

It appears that Machaa was a man of prudence, and seeing that a desperate conflict was imminent, he embarked with six chosen followers and his bride, in a large double canoe, and with plenty of provisions sailed in the night for some more genial clime. The great spirit "Meke-Meke" is supposed to have appeared to him and made it known that a large uninhabited island could be found by steering towards the setting sun. The land was sighted after they had been out two months, and the canoe was beached on the south side of the island. On the second day after their arrival they found a turtle on the beach near Anekena, and one of the men was killed by a blow of its flipper in trying to turn it over. Two months after they had landed on the island, the two canoes with Hotu-Matua and his followers, three hundred in number, arrived.

The desertion of Machaa did not appease the wrath of Oroi, and war to the death was carried on until Hotu-Matua, after being defeated in three great battles, was driven to the last extremity. Discouraged by his misfortune, and convinced that his ultimate capture and death were certain, he determined to flee from the island of Marae-toe-hau, and accordingly had two large canoes, 90 feet long and 6 feet deep, provisioned and prepared for a long voyage. In the night, and on the eve of another battle, they sailed away, with the understanding that the setting sun was to be their compass.

It appears that the intended flight of Hotu-Matua was discovered by Oroi at the last moment, and that energetic individual smuggled himself on board of one of the canoes, disguised as a servant. After arriving upon the island, he hid himself among the rocks at Orongo, and continued to seek his revenge by murdering every unprotected person who came in his way. This interesting state of affairs continued for several years, but Oroi was finally captured in a net thrown by Hotu-Matua and was pounded to death. The tradition continues by a sudden jump into the following extraordinary condition of affairs: Many years after the death of Hotu-Matua, the island was about equally divided between his descendants and the "long-eared race," and between them a deadly feud raged. Long and bloody wars were kept up, and great distress prevailed on account of the destruction and neglect of the crops. This unsatisfactory state of affairs was brought to an end, after many years' fighting, by a desperate battle, in which the "long ears" had planned the utter annihilation of their enemies. A long and deep ditch was dug across Hoto-iti and covered with brush-wood, and into this the "long ears" arranged to drive their enemies, when the brush-wood was to be set on fire and every man exterminated. The trap was found out, and the plan circumvented by opening the battle prematurely and in the night. The "long ears" were driven into the ditch they had built, and murdered to a man.

After the defeat and utter annihilation of the "long-eared race," the tradition goes on to state that peace reigned on the island, and the people increased in numbers and prosperity. In the course of time dissensions arose between the different families or clans, which led to open hostilities. Kaina, the chief of the Hotu-iti clan, and a descendant of the sixth son of the first king, proved himself a valiant warrior, and his possessions were increased by encroachments upon the domain of his neighbors. He died and was succeeded by his son, Huriavai, who inaugurated his introduction into the office by a three days' engagement, in which the chiefs of two neighboring clans were killed. Several clans now combined forces, and after desperate fighting the Hotu-iti people were defeated, half of them taking refuge in a cave on the face of the cliff on the northeast side of the island, and the rest on the islet of Marotiri.

The besieged parties were watched night and day by their vigilant enemies, and were finally reduced to the verge of starvation. A chief, named Poya, had just finished a large double canoe at Hanga-roa, which he called Tuapoi. This was dragged across the island and launched at Anahava. Every day this canoe, filled with fighting men, cruised around the islet of Maroiri, making attacks upon the besieged Hotu-iti people whenever opportunity offered. As the people were reduced by privations, the number of prisoners captured increased day by day. The captives were taken to a place called Hanga-wi-aihi-toke-rau and portioned out to the different clans, and were immediately cooked and eaten. This is said to be the origin of cannibalism on the island, and is supposed to have been prompted by revenge.

Cannibalism, however, proved a double-pointed sword that caused dissensions in the ranks, and finally resulted in the liberation of a part of the besieged people. A chief named Oho-taka-tore happened to be absent upon one occasion, and upon his return found the bodies had all been distributed and his claims completely ignored. He demanded his share of the spoils, and was informed that "a man who sleeps late in the morning can not expect to see the sun rise." Feeling degraded by the slight, Oho-taka-tore turned his feather-hat hind-side before, to indicate that the alliance was broken, and with his men marched off the field.

On the road he stopped at Vaka-piko, at the house of his daughter-in-law, to inquire after his son. The "lady" received him with demonstrations of respect, and while listening to the story of his wrongs, stood behind him and picked fleas out of his head, which, in accordance with the native customs, was the most delicate compliment that one individual could show another.

Upon the return of her husband, whose name was Moa, the woman related the particulars of the visit of his father. Moa said nothing about the state of his feelings, but arose at sunrise and dug up a lot of potatoes and yams, which he baked in an oven. Towards evening he brought out his fish-net and employed himself in arranging the floats and sinkers. After dark he wrapped up his potatoes and yams in sugar-cane and leaves, shouldered his net, and started off, after informing his wife that he was going fishing. He hid his net in the rocks at Kahiherea and then went to Mounga-tea-tea, where a palm tree was growing, from which he cut and trimmed eight large branches. At Ngana Moa he found the camp of the men who guarded the cliff overlooking the cave where the Hotu-iti people were imprisoned, so he turned and went down by the sea-shore. The men stationed there to guard the approach were all asleep, and Moa managed by great caution to pass them without being discovered. Having arrived near the cave he was challenged, and replied, "I am Moa, who seeks revenge while helping you." One of the besieged men, named Tokihai, descended from the cave and received the grip of friendship by being clasped around the belly. Moa took his food into the cave and distributed it among the thirty famished and thoroughly discouraged men who remained alive.

While the great canoe was making its predatory excursions to the islet, the combined forces had not neglected the people who had taken refuge in the cave. Every day a large net filled with men was lowered from the top of the cliff, and from it stones were hurled into the cave, killing and maiming the defenseless people. Moa produced his palm branches and instructed his friends how to make hooks from pieces of human bone, which could be fastened to the poles and used as grapples.

Before daylight everything was in readiness, and when the net was lowered abreast of the opening, it was caught by the hooks and drawn in the cave, and the men in it dispatched almost without resistance. The prisoners got into the net and were hoisted to the top, where by reason of the surprise and the fierceness of their fighting their enemies were defeated and put to flight.

It happened that on the night of Moa's visit to the cave, Huriarai and a man named Vaha, who were with the party on the small island of Marori, became desperate from hunger and made an effort to capture one of the men guarding the sea-beach. The sentry saw one of the men swimming towards him; it proved to be the chief Huriarai, who was so much exhausted that he was clubbed to death without making much resistance. Vaha, however, landed some distance off, and creeping upon the sentry killed him while he was bending over the body of his victim. Vaha hastily buried the body of his chief among the rocks and taking his victim upon his back swam back to his companions on the islet. The people there were without means of making a fire and the body had to be eaten raw. In the morning, when they saw the escape of their comrades from the cave and the desperate fighting on the cliff, they all swam ashore and joined forces.

The traditions, from this point, are a record of tribal wars, abounding in feats of personal bravery and extraordinary occurrences, but of little value to the history of the island. The discovery of the island by Hotu-Matua and his band of three hundred, together with the landing already referred to, is probably correct and seems natural enough down to the division of the land and the death of the first king. The wars and causes that led to the migration of the people from that unknown land, called Marae-toe-hau, are no doubt based upon a foundation of facts. There is no good reason for doubting the description of the climate of their former home, which would, if accepted, locate it somewhere about the equator, or at all events in the tropics. The heat could not be the effect of volcanic action, or their legends would not state that the crops were burned up by the sun at certain seasons.

The improbable, not to say impossible, part of the story comes in, where Machaa steals away and lands upon the same island which his brother's party reach two months later, by simply steering towards the setting sun. There is not one chance in a million, that two canoes could sail for thousands of miles, steering by such an uncertain and indefinite course, and strike the same little island. The tradition states that Hotu-Matua found the island uninhabited, and immediately contradicts this, by the ridiculous story of his brother and his followers having been there two months. It is not unlikely that the natives, anxious to maintain the credit of the discovery of the island, attempt to account for the presence of an earlier people in this way. This might account for the killing of one of Machaa's men by the turtle, for it has no possible bearing upon the story, beyond the fact that it would account for Hotu-Matua finding a tomb or burial-place on the beach at Anekena, when he first landed.

The story of Oroi disguising himself as a servant and sailing for months in an open canoe, filled with naked savages, without his identity being discovered, is too absurd to be considered, beyond ascribing an origin to the enemy or enemies who murdered Hotu-Matua's people, and whose stronghold was on the rocky cliffs near Orongo. One peculiar feature of the tradition is the allusion to the fighting-net, which must have been something after the fashion of those used in old Roman times. These nets are represented to have been square and weighted at the corners with stones. A lanyard was fastened to the center, and the net was thrown over an antagonist, who was beaten to death while entangled in its meshes. It is worthy of remark that nothing of this sort has been discovered among the Polynesians or their contemporaries on the coast of America.

The suddenness with which the tradition jumps into the warfare between the descendants of the first king and the "long-eared race" is startling, because no previous reference has been made to such a race on the island. It is hardly possible that the "long-ears" were descended from people who landed with them on the island, for those that came with Hotu-Matua were of the same clan, and it is fair to presume that the same customs obtained among them all. Besides, the legends all make a distinction between the "long-eared" race and the descendants of the first king. The "long-ears" appear to have been a power in the land at an early period in the history of the island, though they were eventually defeated and exterminated by the others.

It is possible that there has been more than one migration of people to the island, and that their traditions have been mingled together, but there can be no reasonable doubt about the progenitors of the present islanders being of the Malayo-Polynesian stock. It is difficult to account for the statement, so frequently repeated throughout the legends, that Hotu-Matua came from the eastward and discovered the land by steering towards the setting sun, because the chart shows no islands in that direction which would answer the description of "Marae-toe-hau."

TRADITION REGARDING OBSIDIAN SPEAR-POINTS.

The implements of warfare brought to the island by King Hotu-Matua and his followers were few in number, and in the course of time became broken, lost, or destroyed. The clans were continually at war with each other, but from the want of proper weapons the most desperate encounters resulted in little loss of life. Spears were improvised with heads made of the sharp edges of the calabash, but they proved inefficient weapons and did little execution. During the reign of Aturaugi, the sixth king, a man living near the crater of the Rana Kau, while returning to his home after sundown from Temanevai, where he and his companions had been engaged in a useless struggle, stepped in the darkness upon a sharp stone that cut his foot like a knife. He carried the stone home with him, and in the morning found it to be black volcanic glass, which upon being broken showed vitreous edges such as had cut his foot. Believing he had discovered an effective material for the manufacture of spear-heads, he substituted the obsidian for the calabash points and went forth to meet his enemies. The new weapon proved more puissant than he had hoped for, and havoc was created in the ranks of his opponents. Armed with spear-heads obtained from the obsidian mountain Orito, the discoverer and his clan swept everything before them until the new material became known to all the people. Since the time of this discovery the encounters of the islanders are characterized as more sanguinary.

TRADITION REGARDING FISH HOOKS.

In the time of Atua Ure Rangi, the seventeenth king, the image-makers were exempt from all other kinds of work, and the fishermen were taxed for their chief support. The fish-hooks in use were made of stone, so hard that many months of chipping and grinding were required to fashion one fit for service, and the most perfect hooks, even in the hands of expert fishermen, permitted the escape of a large proportion of the fish. A youth named Urevaiaus, who was descended from a long line of fishermen, living at Hanga Pico, became prominent as one of the most skillful fishermen on the island. His outfit contained hooks bequeathed to him by his forefathers, but he became discouraged by the want of success which he thought his labors demanded, and much time was devoted to a consideration of the subject. One day, after a number of large and choice fish had escaped from his hooks, he determined to spend the entire night in the worship of the god Mea Kabi. About midnight, while he was still at his devotions, the spirit of an ancient fisherman named Tirakoka appeared, and made known the fact that his want of success was due to the inefficiency of the hooks. The spirit directed him to go to the cave in which his father's remains had been interred, and secure a piece of the thigh-bone, out of which a proper hook might be constructed. Urevaiaus became so much frightened by his interview with the spirit, that he failed to remember fully all the instructions that had been given, but he went to the cave the next day and secured the thigh-bone of his paternal parent. For many days he went out in his canoe regularly, but instead of fishing, his entire attention was devoted to the manufacture of an improved hook. During this period his boat returned empty every evening, and his want of success excited the open ridicule of his companions and the concern of his friends, but he persevered until he had fashioned a bone-hook with barbed point.

When ready to test his new invention, a place was selected at a distance from his companions, and his boat was quickly filled with the finest fish. The extraordinary success of the young fisherman, in time excited the envy and jealousy of his companions, and his persistent refusal of all inducements to part with the secret led to a serious quarrel and bitter enmity. A sudden attack was finally planned upon Urevaiaus while at work upon the fishing-grounds; in the effort to preserve his secret the youth lost his life, but the new form of hooks was found in his boat and the invention became known to the fraternity.

GENEALOGY OF THE KINGS OF EASTER ISLAND.

Hotu-Matua, driven from his kingdom to the eastward by the rebellion of his subjects, landed with a chosen band of followers at Easter

Islands, in the month of August (Anekena), in two canoes, each 15 fathoms long and 1 fathom deep.

First. Hotu Matua.
Second. Tuumaeheke.
Third. Nuku.
Fourth. Miru.
Fifth. Hiuarirn.
Sixth. Aturaugi.
Seventh. Raa.
Eighth. Atarauga.
Ninth. Hakapuna.
Tenth. Oihu.
Eleventh. Ruhoi.
Twelfth. Tukauga te Mamaru.
Thirteenth. Takahita.
Fourteenth. Ouarna.
Fifteenth. Korobarua.
Sixteenth. Mahuta Ariiki.*
Seventeenth. Atua Ure Raugi.
Eighteenth. Teriri Turkura.
Nineteenth. Korua-Rougo.
Twentieth. Tiki-Tebatu.
Twenty-first. Urukeuu.
Twenty-second. Terurnatiki te Hatu.
Twenty-third. Nau Ta Mahiki.
Twenty-fourth. Terika Tea.
Twenty-fifth. Teria Kautahito.
Twenty-sixth. Kotepu Ite Toki.
Twenty-seventh. Kote Hiti Ruanea.
Twenty-eighth. Turna Ki Keua.
Twenty-ninth. Tuterkimauara.

Thirtieth. Kote Kura Tahoua.
Thirty-first. Taoraha Kaihahauga.
Thirty-second. Tukuma.
Thirty-third. Tekahui te Hunga.
Thirty-fourth. Tetun Hunga Nui.
Thirty-fifth. Tetun Hunga Roa.
Thirty-sixth. Tetu Hunga Mare Kapeau.†
Thirty-seventh. Toati Rangi Hahe.†
Thirty-eighth. Tagaroa Tatarara.
Thirty-ninth. Harini Koro.
Fortieth. Puuahuko.
Forty-first. Puna Ate Tuu.
Forty-second. Puna Kai te Vaua.
Forty-third. Teriri Katea.
Forty-fourth. Hanmoana.
Forty-fifth. Tupaarii Ki.
Forty-sixth. Mahiki Tapuakiti.
Forty-seventh. Tuu Koiho.
Forty-eighth. Anekena.
Forty-ninth. Nui Tupahotu.
Fiftieth. Re Kanu.
Fifty-first. Terava Rara.
Fifty-second. Tehitehuke.
Fifty-third. Terahoi.
Fifty-fourth. Kaimokoi.
Fifty-fifth. Ngaara.
Fifty-sixth. Kaimakoi Iti.
Fifty-seventh. Maurata.

Maurata, the last king, only reigned three years. He was carried away by the Peruvians in 1864, and it is supposed to have died in the guano mines of the Chinchi Islands.

LIST OF ETHNOGRAPHIC SPECIMENS OBTAINED AT EASTER ISLAND.

Wooden image.—Called Moai Tangata. Male figure made of toromiro wood, with eyes of bone and obsidian. (Plate L, fig. 1.)

Wooden image.—Called Moai Kva-kva. Male figure made of toromiro wood, with eyes of bone and obsidian, and breast-bone and ribs sharply defined. (Plate L, fig. 2.)

Wooden image.—Called Moai Papaa. Female figure made of toromiro wood, with eyes of bone and obsidian. (Plate L, fig. 3.)

These figures have been called household gods, and were never worshipped, though they were regarded as the representations of certain spirits. Similar figures were made to represent deceased chiefs and

---

* Mahuta Ariiki had a son named Tuu-Koiho, who made the first stone image on the Island. This son died before his father.

† These two kings reigned at the same time. The son rebelled against his father, and finally killed him.

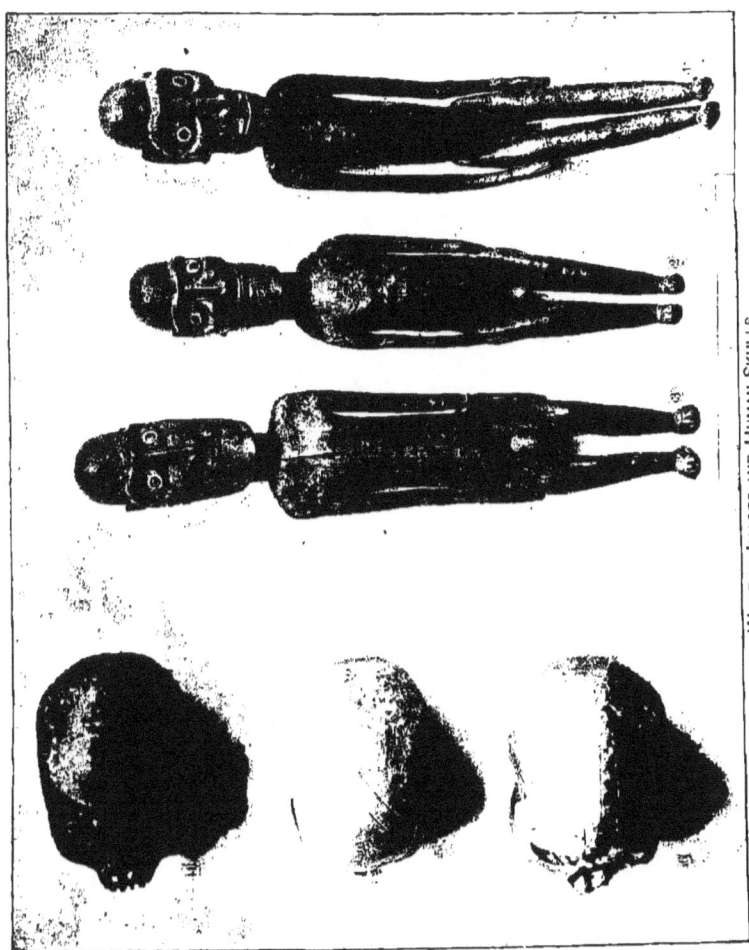

WOODEN IMAGES AND HUMAN SKULLS.

Figs. 1, 2, 3. WOODEN IMAGES. (Cat. Nos. 129743-129745, U. S. N. M. Easter Island. Collected by Paymaster W. J. Thomson, U. S. N.)
Figs. 4, 5, 6. HUMAN SKULLS. (Cat. No. 129759, U. S. N. M. Easter Island. Collected by Paymaster W. J. Thomson, U. S. N.)

Report of National Museum, 1889.—Thomson. PLATE LI.

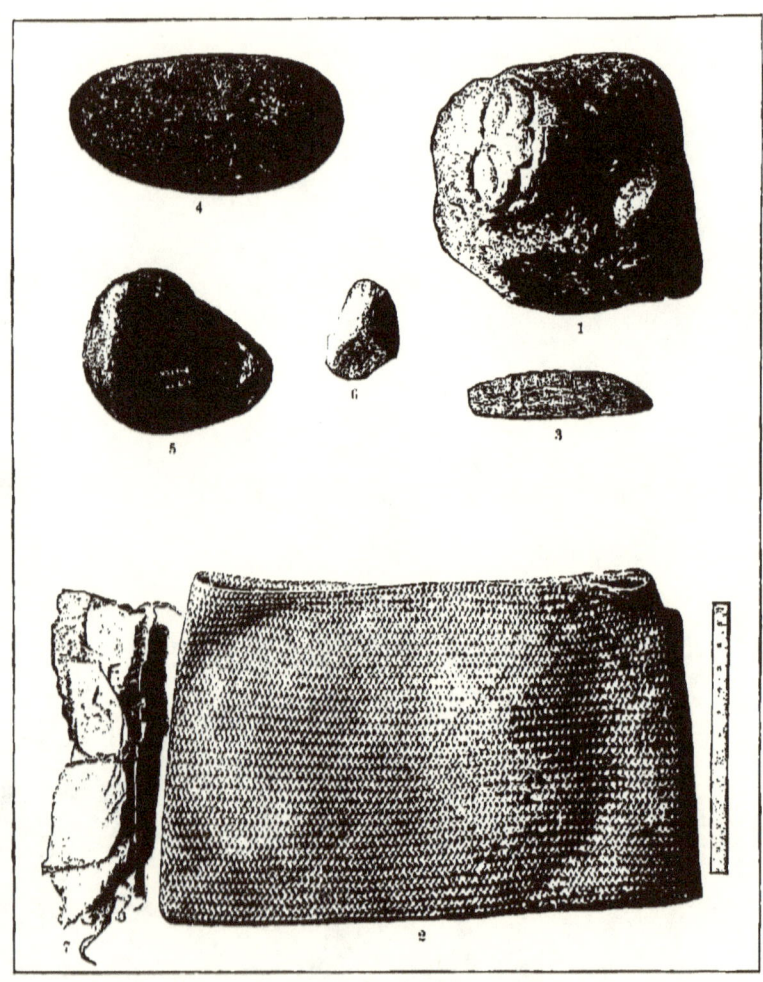

STONE GODS, BULRUSH WALLET, ETC.

Figs. 1, 4, 5, 6. STONE GODS. (Cat. Nos. 129770-129773, U. S. N. M. Easter Island. Collected by Paymaster W. J. Thomson, U. S. N.)

Fig. 2. BULRUSH WALLET. (Cat. No. 129760, U. S. N. M. Easter Island. Collected by Paymaster W. J. Thomson, U. S. N.)

Fig. 3. KNIFE. (Cat. No. 129735, U. S. N. M. Easter Island. Collected by Paymaster W. J. Thomson, U. S. N.)

Fig. 7. TAPOA-CLOTH. (Cat. No. 129739, U. S. N. M. Easter Island. Collected by Paymaster W. J. Thomson, U. S. N.)

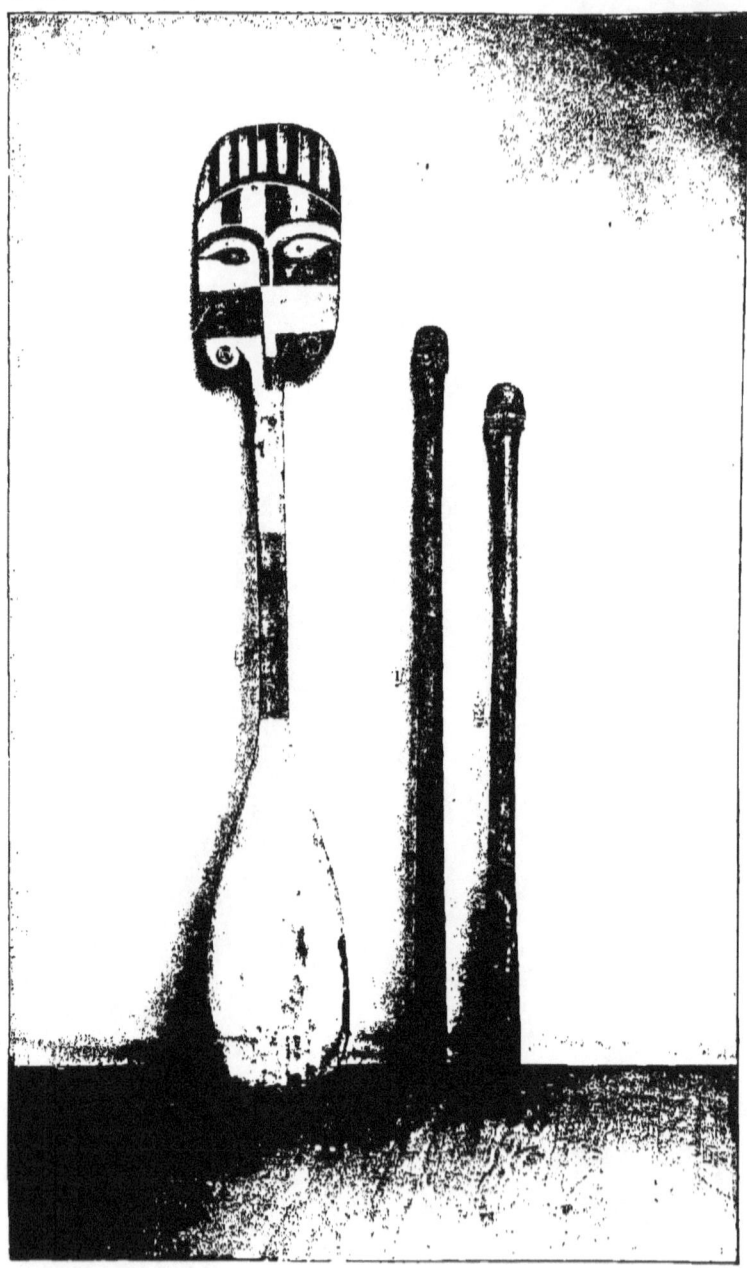

WOODEN CLUBS AND PADDLE.

Figs. 1, 2. WOODEN CLUBS. (Cat. No. 129761, U. S. N. M. Easter Island. Collected by Paymaster W. J. Thomson, U. S. N.)

Fig. 3. PADDLE. (Cat. No. 129749, U. S. N. M. Easter Island. Collected by Paymaster W. J. Thomson. U. S. N.)

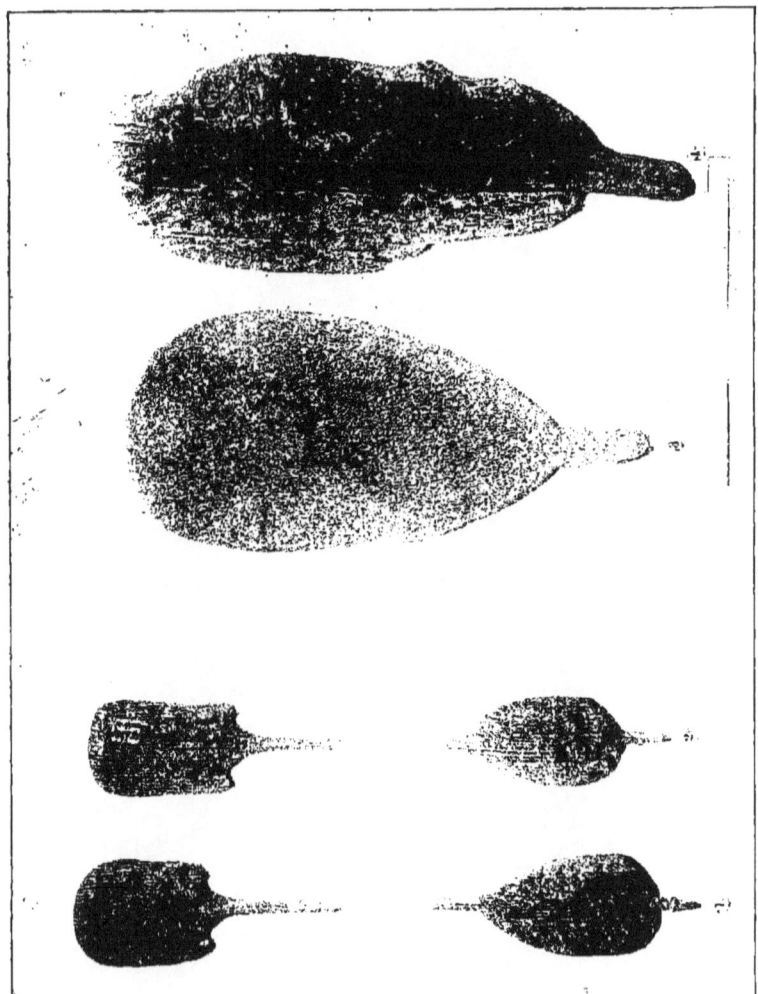

DANCING WANDS AND FETISH BOARDS.

FIGS. 1, 2. DANCING WANDS. (Cat. No. 129540, U. S. N. M. Easter Island. Collected by Paymaster W. J. Thomson, U. S. N.)
FIGS. 3, 4. FETISH BOARDS. (Cat. Nos. 129541-129542, U.S.N.M. Easter Island. Collected by Paymaster W. J. Thomson, U. S. N.)

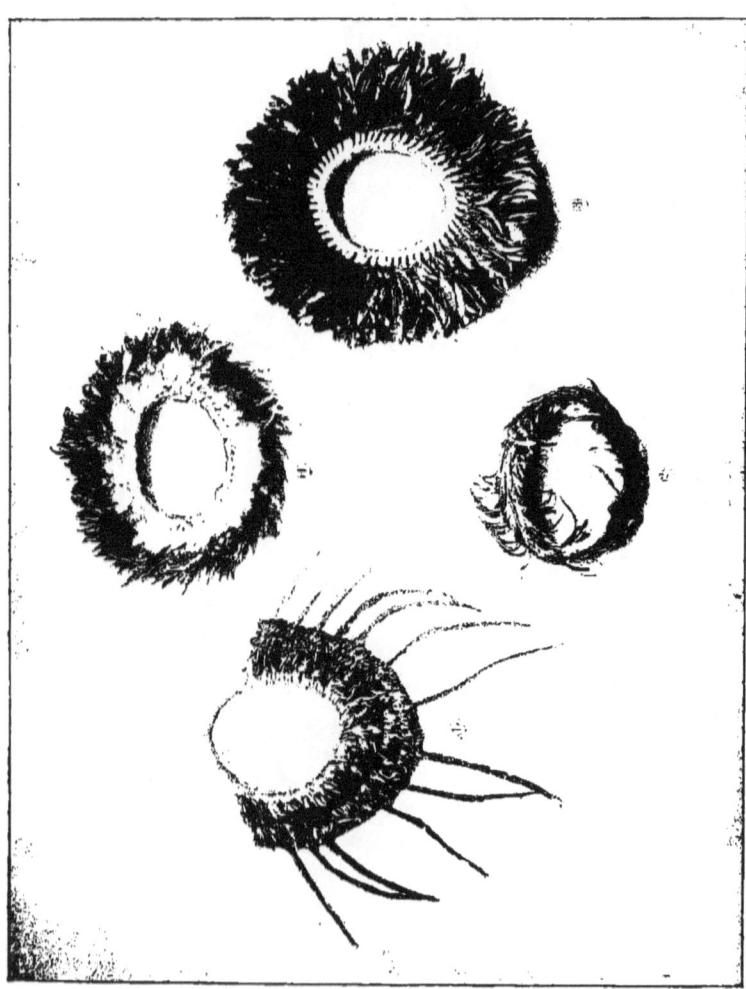

FEATHER HATS.

persons of note, and were given a place of honor at feasts and ceremonies.

Stone image.—Called Moai Maea. Male figure; held in the same estimation as those made of wood. (Plate LI, fig. 1.)

Wooden clubs.—Called Ua. Made of toro-miro wood, 6 feet long, the point slightly widened and the handle ornamented with a bi-fronted head with eyes of bone and obsidian. These clubs were only used as batôns of office by the chiefs, and the handle was supposed to represent the effigy of the owner. (Plate LII, figs. 1 and 2.)

Wooden club.—Called Poa. Made of heavy wood, about 30 inches long, gradually widened from the handle to a broad blade, rounded at the end. These were used for fighting and were handled with great dexterity.

Wooden club.—Called Ao. Made of light wood, used as wands in dancing. The flattened ends are sometimes ornamented with heads supposed to represent females noted for skill and grace in this accomplishment. (Plate LIII, figs. 1 and 2.)

Wooden club.—Called Ariiki. Made of toro-miro wood, the end being turned at right angles from the short handle. The club is ornamented all over with heads. This was the batôn of the king and used only by him. Obtained with much difficulty and expense.

Calabash.—Called Hue Vai. Opened at the small end only, used as a water vessel, and for domestic purposes.

Calabash.—Called Epu Moa. Known as the fowl gourd, and a superstition ascribes a beneficial influence over the chickens fed and watered from it.

Calabash.—Called Tata. Used chiefly in boats for bailing.

Calabash.—Very old specimen obtained from an ancient tomb, covered with hieroglyphics similar to those found on the incised tablets. These calabashes grow in profusion on the island, but are worthy of note on account of the prominent place they occupy in the traditions, and because the seed was introduced by the original settlers.

Fish-net.—Called Kupenga Maito. This form of net has been in use from an early period, and is made from the fiber of wild hemp. Nets of different sizes used in fishing, as well as those for fighting and other purposes, were of similar material and mesh. (Plate XIII.)

Feather hat.—Called Vana-vana. Head-dress made of black and green variegated feathers, used only in delivering a challenge to combat for revenge. (Plate LIV, fig. 1.)

Feather hat.—Called Hau Kura-kura. Small head-dress of brown or red feathers worn by soldiers in time of war. (Plate LIV, fig. 2.)

Feather hat.—Called Hau Pan-ten-ki. Head-dress of long, black, green, and variegated feathers worn by dancing-people. (Plate LIV, fig. 3.)

Featherhat.—Called Hau Tara. Small head-dress of trimmed feathers ornamented by long tail feathers behind; used by chiefs on occasions of ceremony. (Plate LIV, fig. 4.)

Feather hat.—Called Han Vaero. Head-dress used in dancing, and formerly at marriage feasts. (Plate LV, fig. 1.)

Feather hat.—Called Han Hie-bie. Large and heavy head-dress made of black feathers worn by chiefs as insignia of office. These hats are made of chicken feathers secured by the quill ends to a foundation of knitted hemp, intended to fit the head closely. They are frequently referred to in the traditions. (Plate LV, fig. 2.)

Wallet.—Called Kate. Made from bullrushes taken from the crater of Rana-Kau. (Plate LI, fig. 2.)

Mat.—Called Moenga. Made of bullrushes and used for sleeping mats.

Obsidian spear-points.—Plate LVI.—Large collection showing the nine classes into which they are divided by the natives. Fig. 1, narrow leaf-shaped spear-head, called Mataa Nutakuku. Fig. 2, wide round-pointed spear-head, called Mataa Rei-pure-pure-rova. Fig. 3, narrow and long-pointed spear-head, called Mataa Nebo-mango. Fig. 4, narrow spade-shaped spear-head, called Mataa Hikutiveva. Fig. 5, broad straight-edged spear-head, called Mataa-hae. Fig. 6, smooth round-edged spear-head, called Mataa Aro-kiri. Fig. 7, broad fan-shaped spear-head, called Mataa Nutu-kuku. Fig. 8, concave and convex sided spear-head, called Mataa Roa. Fig. 9, long sharp, irregular pointed spear-head, called Mataa Hai-baerve. These spear-heads were fastened to poles about 8 feet long, by lashings of hemp, and formed the chief weapon used by the natives in their frequent strifes. They were thrown to a distance, as well as a thrusting weapon, much after the manner in which the Zulus use their assagais. The volcanic glass of which the points were made, crops out at many places on the island, but was chiefly obtained at the obsidian mountain of Orito. Spear-heads of different shapes and sizes were dependent upon individual taste and skill. The best samples in the collection were purchased from Mr. Salmon; others were found in the tombs and burial-places; and some were picked up on the old battle-grounds.

Fetish-board.—Called Timoika. Broad, flat paddle made of whale-bone, 30 inches long and 14 inches wide. This wand is used in working a charm against an enemy. The injured individual while performing a sort of convulsive dance, makes mystic movements with the paddle, meanwhile muttering incantations in a monotonous tone. The result is believed to be the speedy death of the person against whom the fetish is invoked. (Plate LIII, fig. 3.)

Potato fetish.—Called Rapa. Small, light paddle double bladed, about 24 inches long, painted light red in color. It was used with appropriate ceremonies at times when the potato crop was in danger from insects or drought, and was believed to ward off and guard against evil spirits. (Plate LIII, fig. 4.)

FEATHER HATS.

(Cat. Nos. 129754-129755, U. S. N. M. Easter Island. Collected by Paymaster W. J. Thomson, U. S. N.)

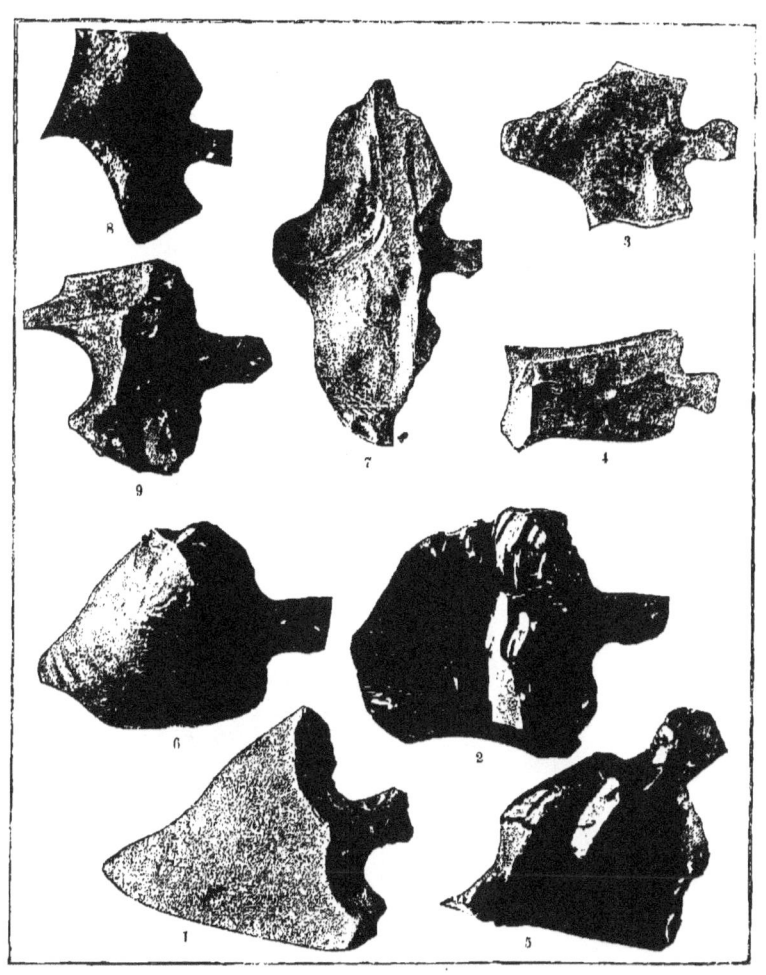

OBSIDIAN SPEAR-HEADS.

(Cat. Nos. 129722-129730, U. S. N. M. Easter Island. Collected by Paymaster W. J. Thomson, U. S. N.)

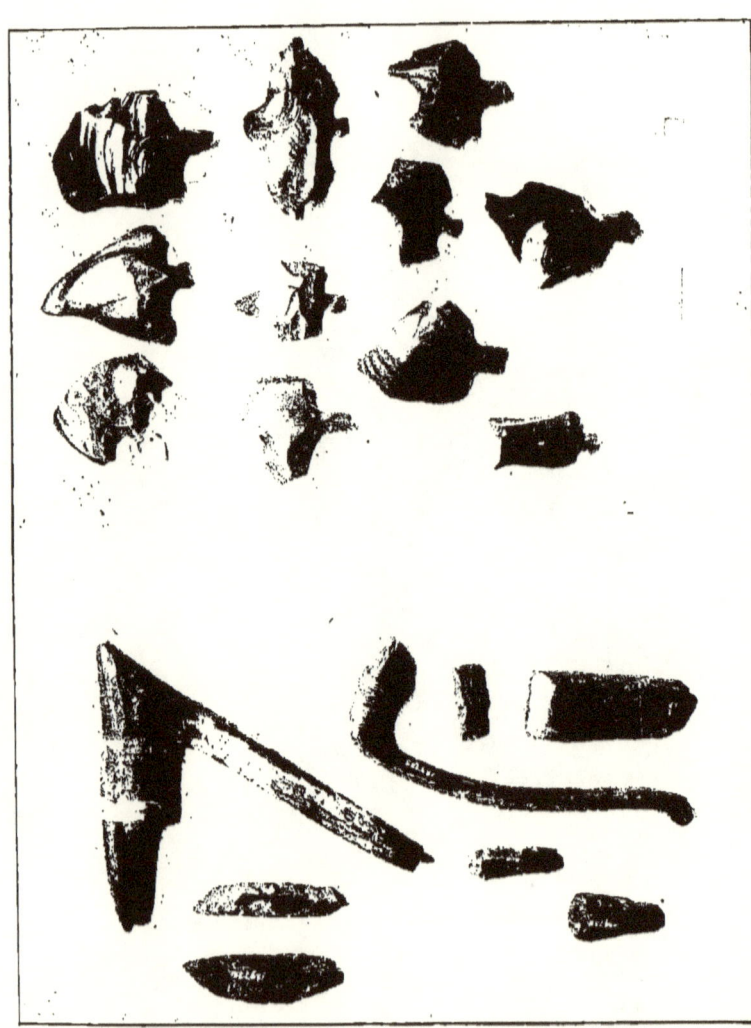

STONE ADZES AND OBSIDIAN SPEAR-HEADS.

STONE ADZES. (Cat. Nos. 129732–129734, U.S.N.M. Easter Island. Collected by Paymaster W. J. Thomson, U.S.N.)
OBSIDIAN SPEAR HEADS. (Cat. Nos. 129722–129730, U.S.N.M. Easter Island. Collected by Paymaster W. J. Thomson, U.S.N.)

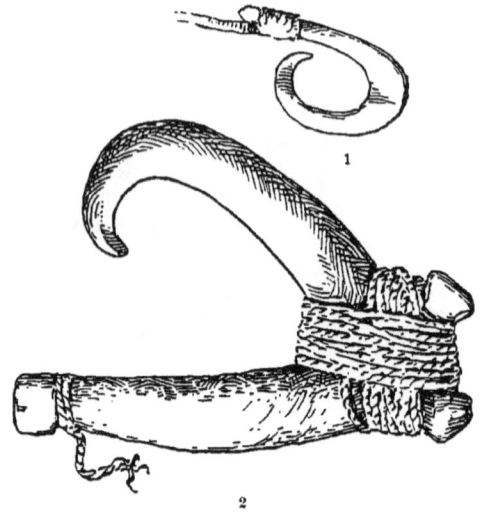
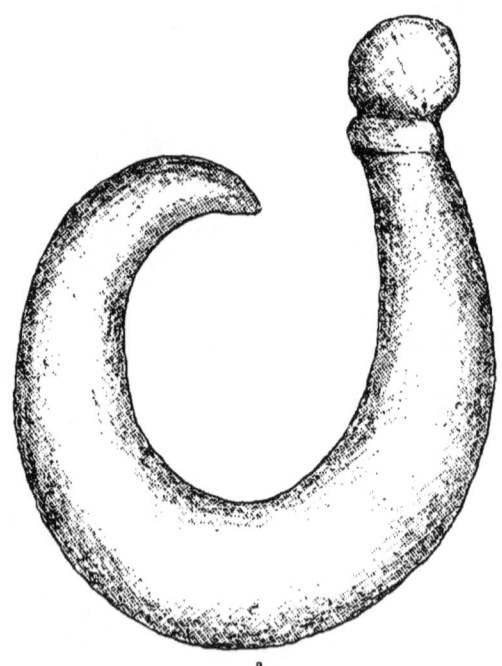

FISHHOOKS.

Fig. 1. FISHHOOK OF HUMAN BONE. (Cat. No. 129736, U. S. N. M. Easter Island. Collected by Paymaster W. J. Thomson, U. S. N.)
Fig. 2. FISHHOOK OF HUMAN BONE. (Cat. No. 129737, U. S. N. M. Easter Island. Collected by Paymaster W. J. Thomson, U. S. N.)
Fig. 3. FISHHOOK OF STONE.

Stone adzes.—Called Toki. The collection comprises twenty-five different sizes, called by distinctive names which signify the use for which they are designed. Tools of this class were always used in a wooden handle. (Plate LVII.)

Stone knife.—Called Hoe. Ground down to a knife-blade with a point and cutting edge, used principally for fashioning the eyes and faces of the images. (Plate LI, fig. 3.)

Ax handles.—Miro Toki. Hard-wood, with natural joint, used for holding stone implements. (Plate LVII.)

Fish god.—Called Mea Ika. This rough, ill-shaped stone was one of the objects really worshipped by the natives. Some of them bear evidences of tool marks, but it does not appear that any effort was made to carve them into shape or decorate them. These gods were never common, and were possessed by communities or clans, and not by individuals. The legends claim that they were all brought to the island by Hotu Matua and the first settlers. (Plate LI, fig. 4.)

Bonito god.—Called Mea Kahi. A stone with apparently no distinguishing characteristics, and nothing to merit the profound religious homage paid to it. It is not clear why the bonito should have the distinction of a separate god from the other fish, unless it be for the reason that it appears in great numbers in these waters, and has always been highly esteemed as an article of food. Fish always constituted an important diet with the natives, and the abundance in which they were found was ascribed to the faithful and constant adoration of these stone gods. (Plate LI, fig. 5.)

Fowl god.—Called Mea Moa. A beach pebble with slight traces of tool-marks, but it might readily be passed among other stones without attracting attention. To the fowl god is ascribed the custody of chickens, and its beneficial influence was secured by being placed under a setting hen for a short time before the eggs were hatched. (Plate LI, fig. 6.)

Stone Fish Hook.—Called Mugai Kihi. These primitive hooks, now very rare on the island, were made of the hardest rock to be obtained, and were ground into shape by long and constant rubbing. (Plate LVIII, fig. 3.)

Bone fish-hooks.—Called Mugai Iri. In accordance with an ancient superstition, these hooks were manufactured from the thigh-bones of deceased fishermen. The curve was fashioned with a small barb which prevented the escape of the fish. The form is so perfectly adapted to the purpose that the natives still use their old bone hooks in preference to those of European make. A fish-hook of similar design was used by the Indians of Santa Cruz Island. (Plate LVIII, figs. 1 and 2.)

Incised tablets.—Called Hokau Rongo-Rongo. Two specimens in excellent state of preservation, showing the hieroglyphics used in the written language. (Plates XXXVIII–XLI.)

Double paddle.—Called Mata Kao-kao. Made of heavy wood, balanced by wide blades ornamented with outlined faces. Used in the ancient canoes in a similar manner to that practiced by the Indians of America. (Plate LII, fig. 3.)

Ancient scull oars —Called Mata Kao. Angular float of peculiar shape and unique design attached to a long handle. Used for steering and sculling very large canoes. Very old and highly prized by the islanders as the only specimen of the scull-oar used by their ancestors. (Plate LIX.)

Human skulls.—Called Puoko Iri. An examination of these skulls shows very little difference between the crania of the present people and those found in the most ancient tombs. Three specimens obtained from the King's platform have hieroglyphics engraved upon them, which signify the clan to which they belonged. (Plate L.)

Native cloth.—Called Hami Nua. Made of the inner bark of the hibiscus and paper-mulberry trees. The manufacture of the "tappa" has now ceased altogether. (Plate LI, fig. 7.)

Tattooing implements.—Called Ta Kona. Tools used for puncturing the skin. Made of bird bones.

Needles.—Called Iri. Both bone and wooden needles used for sewing tappa cloth, and other varieties for knitting meshes of nets. (Plate LX, fig. 1.)

Fetish stones.—Called Atua Mangaro. A collection obtained by digging beneath the door-posts of the ancient dwellings. The majority are simply beach pepples; others have been formed by rubbing; and one is a triangular-shaped stone with a face outlined upon it. These were placed beneath the houses, with much ceremony, and were supposed to ward off evil influences. (Plate LX, fig. 2.)

Neck ornaments.—Called Hoko Ngao. Carved wood in fanciful designs worn during the dance.

Pigments.—Called Penetuli. Natural paints used by being ground down in the heated juice of the sugar cane.

Frescoed slabs.—Taken from the inner walls and ceilings of the stone houses at Orongo. (Plate XXIII.)

Fetish stones.—Buried under the corner-stones of the houses.

POLYNESIAN ARCHÆOLOGY.

The most ancient monuments of Polynesia are the lithic and megalithic remains, coincident in style and character with the Druidical circles of Europe, and the exact counterpart of those of Stonehenge and Carnac in Brittany. These earlier efforts of the human art are invariably the remains of temples, places of worship, or of edifices dedicated in some way to the religion and superstitions of extinct generations, whose graves cover every island and reef. The most numerous, and perhaps the most ancient structures, are quadrangular in shape, and are composed of loose lava stones, forming a wall of great firmness and strength. These temples frequently exceed 100 feet in length, with a

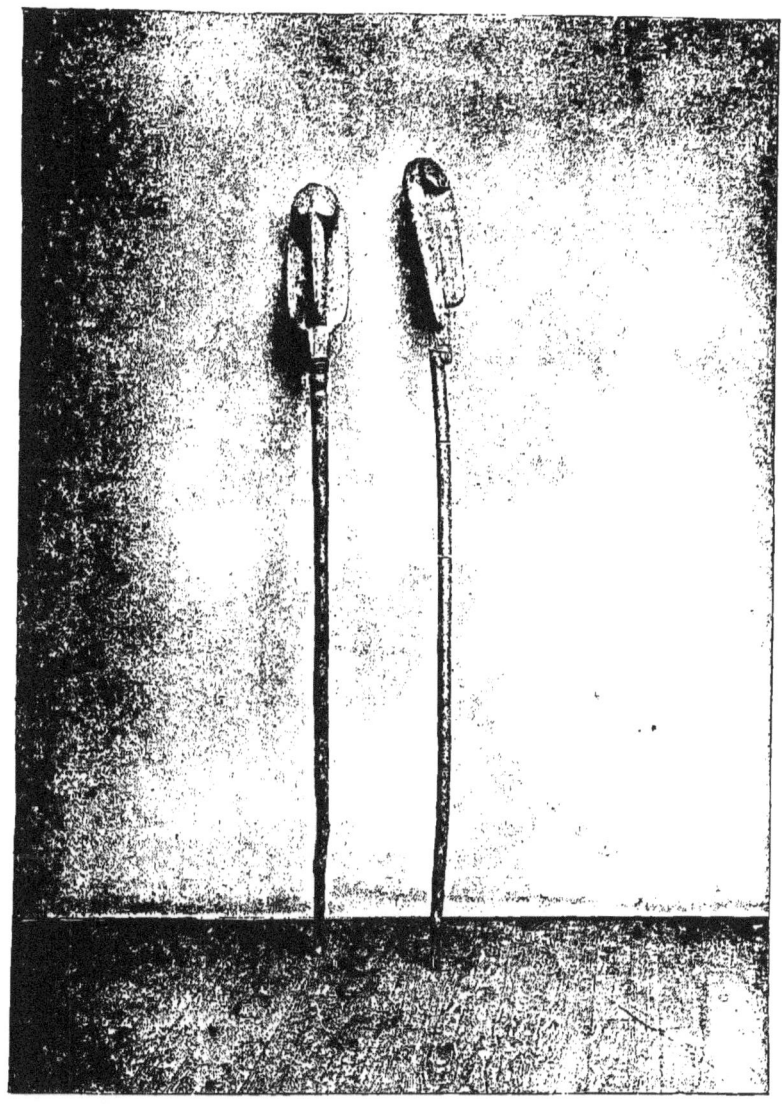

ANCIENT SCULL-OARS.

(Cat. No. 129746, U. S. N. M. Easter Island. Collected by Paymaster W. J. Thomson, U. S. N.)

Report of National Museum, 1889.—Thomson. PLATE LX.

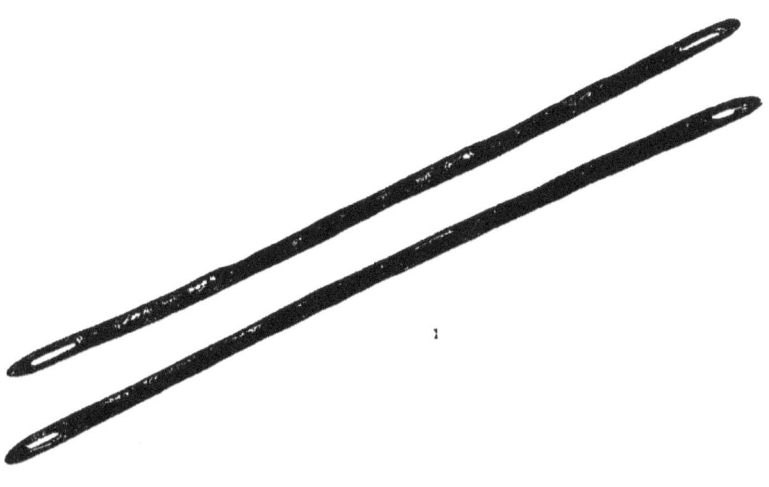

NETTING-NEEDLES AND FETISH-STONES.

Fig. 1. NETTING-NEEDLES. (Cat. No. 129738, U. S. N. M. Easter Island. Collected by Paymaster W. J. Thomson, U. S. N.)
Fig. 2. FETISH-STONES. (Cat. Nos. 129765-129772, U. S. N. M. Easter Island. Collected by Paymaster W. J. Thomson, U. S. N.)

proportionate width, and were designed to be roofless. They contain remains of altars composed of the same materials as the wall of the main inclosure, generally located at one end, and in shape resembling parallelograms. In many cases, these edifices are in as perfect a state of preservation as when countless numbers of human victims were immolated upon their altars, though time has obliterated all traces of everything perishable.

In the search for prehistoric remains, the diversified character of the many islands that dot the South Sea should be borne in mind. Coral groups and atolls, these wonderful formations produced by the ceaseless work of zoöphytic animals, being of comparatively recent creation, were perhaps merely tide-water reefs, when the islands of purely volcanic character were peopled by lawless and turbulent tribes, constantly engaged in warfare and in making depredations upon each other. Even where there is sufficient evidence of antiquity to warrant the search, the absence of monuments upon the low-lying islands of coral formation, may be accounted for by the lack of suitable material for their construction, or to the destroying hurricanes that occasionally sweep across this part of the Pacific, which are accompanied by a furious sea that breaks completely over the narrow atolls, carrying death and devastation to all things animate and inanimate.

The height of the atolls, in many cases, does not exceed 5 or 6 feet above the normal level of the sea surrounding them, and instances are unfortunately abundant, of islands that have been transformed in a few hours, from a scene of tropical luxuriance and with a contented people surrounded by nature's most bountiful gifts, to one of utter barrenness and desolation. The largest and most important islands of Polynesia are of volcanic character, and bear evidences of having been inhabited from a remote period. Here may be duplicated the Teocallis of Palenque, Copan, and Uxmal. In some islands these ancient monuments were searched out with great difficulty, having been so completely overgrown with dense tropical vegetation that their existence was not suspected by the indifferent people of to-day.

While the islanders never advanced to a high civilization, and their best efforts consist in cromlechs, dolmens, and elevated platforms or truncated pyramids, their handiwork is still preserved, and points with abundant interest to the history of a rude and early age.

The primitive Polynesians, like their contemporaries, the Incas of Peru, may be judged in regard to their condition and history, by the monuments they have left, for with the exception of Easter Island, there is no trace of their having possessed a written language. Tribes flourished, were conquered and passed out of existence, without leaving a trace behind them except perhaps, a shadowy tradition. The natives in this genial climate have always dwelt in rude structures of thatch and cane, which after a few years of abandonment would decay and leave no sign behind, unless it be a few broken implements lying about. Among them, traditions have always been preserved with care, and it is wonderful to find how the history of a people can be followed in this way for hundreds of years. The Samoans claim a complete chronicle dating through twenty-two generations of the reigning family of Malietoa, and extending over a period of eight hundred years, while the Tongans can chronicle a fairly accurate history of their priesthood through twelve centuries.*

The priests have usually been the custodians of the national traditions, and there is sufficient evidence to show that every precaution was taken to have them handed down from one generation to another, pure and unchanged, for oral record was their only means of committing to posterity the deeds of their ancestors.

To be intrusted with the traditions, constituted of itself an office of high dignity, and the holder was afforded the protection of a taboo of the most rigorous character.

Family records were perpetuated with the national history, but as might be expected, there was a tendency to embellish them when extended back beyond a reasonable limit, with mythological personages and improbable occurrences. Still the extraordinary power of these keepers to preserve unimpaired for centuries, events and facts or even the genealogy of important families, would astonish those who are familiar only with written history, and whose memories depend upon artificial aids. Except in a few cases, the traditions of the natives do not extend back far enough to throw much light upon the ancient monuments found upon the islands. This is due in a measure to the fact, that in only isolated localities have the people lived unmolested for any great length of time. The tribes were continually at war with one another. From love of conquest, and jealousy, no tribe was safe from the depredations of its neighbor, although living upon terms of supposed friendship. The love of war induced frequent expeditions planned for the destruction of the tribes of adjacent islands, while occasionally a combination was made for more extensive operations against the unsuspecting natives of a different group. The visitors usually put to death the fighting men of the conquered tribes and absorbed the others. The traditions of both parties were preserved separately for a time, but they naturally tended to merge together, and in this state, a combination of the glories of both tribes were handed down never to be unraveled to their succeeding generations. The monuments of antiquity scattered throughout Polynesia, with the exception of Easter Island, increase in importance as we advance to the westward, commencing with the circles of uncut stones, and advancing by regular steps until we arrive at the more elaborate sculptures. This fact indicates the decline that

---

* These genealogies, although widely known and generally admitted to be true, have received the special investigation of some of the missionaries. The Rev. Shirley Baker, now premier of Tonga, assures us that there is no reason to doubt them, and that on the other hand there are many reasons for accepting them as absolute truth.

took place in the social and mental culture of the people as they ramified eastward through the various islands of the Pacific. Detachments arriving at the different groups separated into distinct communities as accident or fancy directed; here they became segregated, and rapidly degenerated in knowledge and in the arts.

Starting with the Sandwich Islands, we find that the Hawaiian prehistoric remains are confined to the most primitive forms of structures, such as the remains of the pagan temple at Waikiki, and the enormous heiau at Punepa near Iolo, both of which are notable types of walled inclosures, and also the catacombs of Waimea, which do not greatly differ from some of the places of sepulture in other islands.

Farther to the South and West, the Marquesas and Society groups show nothing beyond the primitive works of people who have passed away ages ago, leaving no other signs of their having existed.

The island of Rapa-titi, in mid Pacific and just outside the tropics, contains evidences of a numerous population at some remote period. The island is remarkably mountainous, though quite small, with pinnacles rising to the height of 2,000 feet, and precipitous cliffs jutting into the sea. Massive forts command all the principal valleys; they are constructed of stone; built in terraces; and furnished with towers for observation and rallying points.*

In the Friendly Islands are found some interesting relics of antiquity. Near the ancient metropolis of Moa, on the island of Tongatabu, and about 12 miles from Nukualofa, the present capital of the group, are the graves of the Tui-Tongas.

These embrace nineteen truncated pyramids, measuring about 100 feet square on the base lines, and rising in three terraces to a height of 25 feet. The stones used in their construction are of coral concrete, and many of the huge blocks are 18 feet long by 5½ feet high and 3 feet thick, and weigh fully 20 tons each.

The labor of building these tombs was enormous, and when it is considered that the great blocks were cut from the coral reef about 3 miles distant, and transported to the spot by savages who were ignorant of the laws of mechanics, and who were without appliances, we can not fail to be lost in wonder at the magnitude of the work accomplished. These pyramids are of various ages, extending over a period of twelve hundred and fifty years. They are overgrown by a dense forest of fao and banyan trees, of immense size and great age, the roots of which have dislodged and thrown down some of the largest stones. The Tui-Tongas were high-priests and their genealogy has been carefully preserved.

---

* In 1867, the French purchased the sovereignty of this little island for a gallon of rum and some old clothes, thus cutting out a prospective American Steam-ship Company that had fixed upon it for a coal depot. Coal is found here in small quantities, and this fact has been adduced in support of the theory of a submerged continent in the Pacific, a fallacy evident to the geologist. Although there are several bays, a landing may be made at any point owing to the remarkable smoothness of the sea. The people bear a close resemblance to the New Zealanders.

The priesthood was hereditary, descending from father to son. Under the laws of Tonga the high-priests could marry only the daughters of the king. Their sons became priests, and the daughters occupied a position analogous to that of the Vestal Virgins and were not permitted to marry. This long line is now extinct, the last of the Tui-Tongas having been laid with his fathers in 1863.

About 6 miles beyond these tombs, on the eastern shore, stands an ancient cromlech, or more properly speaking a dolmen. This interesting monument is composed of three blocks of coral concrete. The two uprights are 14 feet high, 8 feet wide and nearly 4 feet thick, and weigh over 15 tons each, while the cross-piece is somewhat smaller and weighs about 10 tons. The native tradition is that these larger masses of stone were cut from the coral reef about 2 miles distant, and that the vertex was brought by one of their large canoes from Wallis Island. While it is possible for this legend to be founded upon fact, there is room for strong doubt, since the same formation exists upon both islands; but the difficulty of handling a stone of that size and weight, and of carrying it a distance of 600 miles by sea, would hardly be warranted when it could be quarried on their own shores. Viewed, however, as a trophy, and the cromlech as a sort of triumphal arch to commemorate a victory, (for the Tongans were perhaps the most successful of the ocean rovers of the Pacific) the legend of the stone seems entitled to greater credence than the neglected pile would at first warrant. The traditions do not go back far enough to tell us by whom this cromlech was erected, but simply assert its erection by one of the early kings on the advent of his dynasty, a fact which the disintegration of the stone, due to age, would seem to corroborate. The Samoans formerly erected stone pillars to the memory of their chiefs, but the most interesting relic of former ages, in this group, is the ruins of a heathen temple located in the mountains near the center of the island of Opolu. Secreted in an almost inaccessible gully, this temple was built in the form of an ellipse, measuring 57 feet one way by 39 feet the other. The roof was evidently thatched with pandanus leaves, as is the custom to the present day, but three large columns of basaltic rock formed the center supports, while the eaves rested upon the pillars of the same stone placed at intervals of 3 feet apart around the ellipse. Many of these stones are still standing, but the site has been almost obscured by a dense tropical growth.

Within a few feet of the old temple is an ancient tomb covered with a large block of stone and marked by an upright basaltic column. Samoan legends do not give much information about this ruin, but the Tongan traditions hold that the temple was built by them, after they had conquered the Samoans, and that the tomb is that of one of the Tui-Tougas who accompanied the successful expedition, and who died and was buried alongside of the temple. This conquest took place at least eight hundred years ago, for it was about this time that Malietoa I. was made king, for his bravery and success in freeing his country from the Tongan yoke.

Plans were made to open this tomb, but for the lack of time could not be carried out, and the observations on this interesting relic were confined to one hasty visit.

Continuing still farther to the westward, to the island of Tinian, one of the Ladrones, are found two ranges of stone columns, over a dozen in number, and somewhat similar in size and shape to those of the cromlech at Tongatabu; but the curious feature of this ruin is that each column is surmounted by a large semi-globe, flat surface upward, weighing 4 tons. Freycinet supposes them to be supports of wooden ceilings to houses, that long ago have fallen into ruin, but other authorities assert that they are sepulchral urns. The natives call them "the houses of the ancients."

Upon the adjacent islands are numerous remains of a similar character, but in most cases the columns are smaller.

In the island of Ponape, Caroline group, are found remains of a higher grade of stone work and which are a puzzle to ethnologists.* Upon the bank of a creek that empties into Metalanien harbor is an inclosure with massive walls built of basaltic prisms 300 feet long and 35 feet high. There is a gateway opening upon the creek composed of enormous basaltic columns laid flat, inside of which is a court inclosed by walls 30 feet high. There are terraces against the wall inside, also built of basaltic prisms 8 feet high and 12 feet wide. The inclosure is nearly square and is divided into three parts by low walls running north and south.

In the center of each court is a closed chamber 14 feet square, ornamented with basaltic columns and roofed with the same stone. On the central ridge of the opposite side of the island, 10 miles distant, are a large number of very fine basaltic columns, and this must have been the quarry for the structure just described, for the configuration of the land is such that roads would have been impracticable, and the only deduction is that the material must have been taken down to the coast and thence by water to the location on the creek.

This is reported to have been the home of the buccaneers, but it is impossible that they could have put up works of such magnitude. There are other ruins on the island, and also some mounds of considerable size, 12 feet high and a quarter of a mile long. On Kusai, and other islands of the group are found ruins, but those of Ponape are by far the most remarkable.

Though not properly in the province of the work, a short description by Mr. Wallace of some of the architectural wonders of Java is inserted. He estimates the date of their construction at five hundred years ago when the island was under the sway of the Hindoos.

---

* From Wallace's "Australia."

The road to Wonosalem led through a magnificent forest, in the depths of which we passed a fine ruin of what appeared to have been a royal tomb or mausoleum. It is formed entirely of stone, and elaborately carved. Near the base is a course of boldly projecting blocks, sculptured in high relief, with a series of scenes which are probably incidents in the life of the defunct. These are all beautifully executed, some of the figures of animals in particular being easily recognizable and very accurate. The general design, as far as the ruined state of the upper part will permit of its being seen, is very good, the effect being given by an immense number and variety of projecting or retreating courses of squared stones in place of mouldings. The size of the structure is about 30 feet square by 20 feet high, and as the traveler comes suddenly upon it on a small elevation by the road side, overshadowed by gigantic trees, overrun with plants and creepers, and closely backed by the gloomy forest, he is struck by the solemnity and picturesque beauty of the scene, and is led to ponder on the strange law of progress, which looks so like retrogression, and which in so many distant parts of the world has exterminated or driven out a highly artistic and constructive race, to make room for one which, as far as we can judge is very far its inferior. The number and beauty of the architectural remains in Java have never been popularly illustrated or described, and it will therefore take most people by surprise to learn that they far surpass those of Central America, perchance those of India. To give some idea of these ruins, perhaps to excite wealthy amateurs to explore them thoroughly, and to obtain by photography an accurate record of these beautiful sculptures before it is too late, I will enumerate the most important as briefly described in Sir Stanforns Raffle's History of Java.

Near the center of Java, between the native capitals of Djoko-Kerta and Sura-Kerta, is the village of Brambanam, not far from which are abundance of ruins, the most important being the temples of Loro-Jongran and Chandi-Sewa. At Loro-Jongran there were separate buildings, six large, and fourteen small temples. They are now a mass of ruins, but the largest temple was supposed to have been 90 feet high. They were all constructed of solid stone, everywhere decorated with carvings and bas-reliefs, and adorned with numbers of statues, many of which remain entire. At Chandi-Sewa, or the "thousand temples," are many fine colossal figures. Captain Baker, who surveyed these ruins, said that he had never in his life seen such stupendous and finished specimens of human labor, and the science and taste of ages long since forgotten, crowded together in so small a compass as in this spot. They cover a span of nearly 600 feet square, and consist of an outer row of eighty-four temples; a second row of seventy-six; a third row of sixty-four; a fourth of forty-four; and a fifth forming an inner parallelogram of twenty-eight; in all two hundred and ninety-six small temples disposed in five regular parallelograms. In the center is a large cruciform temple surrounded by forty flights of steps, richly ornamented with sculpture and containing many apartments.

The tropical vegetation has ruined most of the smaller temples, but some remain tolerably perfect, from which the effects of the whole may be imagined. About half a mile off is another temple, called Chandi Kali Bening, 72 feet square and 60 feet high, in fine preservation, and covered with sculptures of Hindu mythology surpassing any that exists in India. Other ruins of palaces, halls and temples, with abundance of sculptured deities, are found in the same neighborhood.

About 80 miles eastward, in the province of Kedu, is the great temple of Borobods. It is built upon a small hill, and consists of a central dome and seven ranges of terraced wall, covering the slope of the hill, forming open galleries, each below the other, and communicating by steps and gateways. The central dome is 50 feet in diameter; around it is a triple circle of seventy-two towers; and the whole building is 620 feet square and about 100 feet high. In the terraced walls are niches containing cross-legged figures larger than life, to the number of about four hundred; both sides of the terraced walls are covered with bas-reliefs crowded with figures carved in hard stone, which must therefore occupy an extent of nearly 3 miles in length.

The amount of human labor and skill expended upon the great pyramids of Egypt, sink into insignificance when compared with that required to complete this sculptured hill temple in the interior of Java.

About 40 miles southwest of Samarang, on a mountain called Junong Prau, an extensive plateau is covered with ruins. To reach the temples, four flights of stone steps were made up to the mountain from opposite directions, each flight containing more than a thousand steps. Traces of nearly four hundred temples have been found here, and many (perhaps all) were decorated with rich and delicate sculptures. The whole country between this and Brambanam, a distance of 60 miles, abounds with ruins, so that fine sculptured figures may be seen lying in ditches, or built into the walls of inclosures.

In the eastern part of Java, at Kediri, and in Melang, there are equally abundant traces of antiquity, but the buildings themselves have been mostly destroyed; sculptured figures, however, abound, and the ruins of forts, palaces, baths, aqueducts, and temples can be everywhere traced.

The ruins of the ancient city of Majapahit cover miles of ground with paved roads, walls, tombs, and gateways, while sculptures of Hindu gods and goddesses of hard trachytic rock are found in the forests or *in situ* in temples. Some of the buildings are of brick of curious construction; the bricks are burned and built together without cement, and yet adhere incomprehensibly.

LANGUAGE—VOCABULARY.

The natives reckoned their time, and in fact do so still by moons or months, commencing the year with August, which was, according to the traditions, the time when Hotu-Matua and his followers landed upon the island.

The following corresponds nearly to the English months set opposite:

Anekena......August.	Tuaharo......February.
Hora-iti (little summer)......September.	Tetuupu......March.
Hora-nui (big summer)......October.	Tarahao......April.
Tangarouri......part of November.	Vaitu-nui (big winter)......May.
Kotuti......November and December.	Vaitu-poto (short winter)...June.
Ruti......December and January.	Maro or Temaro......July.
Koro......January.	

The natives have recently divided the months into weeks, giving to the days the names of First day (Raa-po-tahi), Second day (Raa-po-rua), Third day (Raa-po-toru), etc. The week is commenced on Monday in order to bring the seventh day on Sunday.

The month is divided into two equal portions, the first beginning with the new moon, and the second with the full moon. The calendar at the time of our visit to the island ran about as follows, the new moon being full on November 26:

Kokore tahi (first Kokore)..November 27	Kokore toru (third Kokore).December 13
Kokore rua (second Kokore).November 28	Kokore há (fourth Kokore).December 14
Kokore toru (third Kokore).November 29	Kokore rima (fifth Kokore)..December 15
Kokore há (fourth Kokore)..November 30	Tapume......December 16
Kokore rima (fifth Kokore).December 1	Matua......December 17
Kokore ono (sixth Kokore)..December 2	Orongo, last quarter......December 18
Maharu, first quarter......December 3	Orongo taane......December 19
Ohua......December 4	Mauri nui......December 20
Otua......December 5	Marui Kero......December 21
Ohotu......December 6	Omutu......December 22
Maure......December 7	Tueo......December 23
Ina-ira......December 8	Oata......December 24
Ra Kau......December 9	Oari, new moon......December 25
Omotohi, full moon......December 10	Kokore tahi (first Kokore)..December 26
Kokore tahi (first Kokore)..December 11	Etc., etc., etc.
Kokore rua (second Kokore).December 12	

The natives of Easter Island speak a dialect of the Malayo-Polynesian language, which is so widely spread in the South Sea and Malay Archipelago. Any one who will take the trouble to compare the accompanying vocabulary with the same words used by the natives of New Zealand, Tahiti, Rorotonga, Samoa, and any of the islands of Polynesia, will see that many of the words are identically the same, and others show a slight variation.

Not only do the words of this language resemble those spoken throughout the South Sea, but all the dialects possess, in common, the peculiarity of having a dual number of the personal pronouns in addition to the singular and plural. For example, he or she is, "Ko-ia," in the Maori it is, "ia;" they two, on this island is "rana-á," in the Maori it is "raua;" they, in this dialect is "pouro," in the Maori, it is "ratou." Words are frequently reduplicated to denote the plural of collectives in nouns, the comparative, or superlative degree in adjectives, and repeated action in verbs. "Iti" signifies little, "iti-iti," expresses very little, and the word for small child is "poki iti-iti." Food, or to eat, is "Kai," to eat much or heartily is expressed by "kai-kai." The names of several of the colors are usually duplicated, as red, "mea-mea;" black, "uri-uri;" white "tea-tea;" vermillion "ura-ura."

An interesting feature of the language is the native name for pig, "Oru," which differs from the corresponding term in all of the other Polynesian dialects. It is probably derived from the grunting sound made by the animal. In nearly all of the kindred dialects the name for pig is "puaka," a word which is also applied by some of them to all quadrupeds except the rat. The Easter Islanders have given this name to cattle, calling a cow "puaka tamahine" (female puaka), and a bull "puaka tamaroa" (male puaka). This tends to show that although pigs had probably been introduced on the islands from which the ancestors of the present inhabitants came, they took none with them in their migration, and only preserved the word puaka in a vague sense, as signifying a large animal with four legs. When cattle were introduced, they consequently applied the term to them, and coined the new one afterwards.

Fingers are called "manga-mauga" and toes, "manga-manga vae," or literally the fingers of the foot. "Kiri" means covering, and to express the wood shoe they say "Kiri vae," or covering, for the foot. "Ivi" is the name applied to both needle and bone, which probably indicates that the original needles were made of bone.

In the pronunciation of words of two syllables, the accent is on the first; in words of three syllables it is generally on the second, and in polysyllabic words it is on the penultimate. Modern articles recently introduced on the island are called by their English names, or something that has a similar sound.

It is worthy of note that the word "Atua" is used to signify both god and devil.

VOCABULARY.

Absent	Ngaro.	A or and	E.
Adieu	Kamoi.	Age	Mata hi.
Air	Haugu.	Abdomen	Manava.
Aid	Haun.	Ankle	Kari-kari vae.
All (whole)	Ananakē.	Arms	Kaufa.
Ancestor	Tupuna.	Arm	Rima.
Artisan	Maori.	Artery	Ua noho toto.
Autumn	Vaha-tonga.	Ash-wood	Mari-kuru.
Ax	Toki.	Ape-fish	Nohue.

Arrow-root	Pia.	Cure	Hakaora.
Bad	Rake-rake.	Cut	Hauva.
Bath	Hopu.	Cut-grass	Kaverimai.
Battle (war)	Tana.	Cape	Heihu.
Bay	Paeonga.	Coat	Lukan.
Before	Vaha.	Come here	Oboginai.
Below	Iraro.	Clay	Oone vai.
Bird	Manu.	Cry	Tangi.
Bird (tropic)	Makohe.	Cattle	Puaka.
Bitter	Kava.	Crab	Pikea.
Black	Uri-uri.	Calf of leg	Reru.
Boat	Vaka Poe-poe.	Chest	Uma.
Boy	Poki-tamaroa.	Chin	Kanae.
Branch	Manga miro.	Clitoris	Matakao.
Bring me	Kotomai.	Copulate	Tuki-tuki.
Brother (younger)	Hangu potu.	Convolvulus	Tauoa.
Brother (elder)	Atariki.	Calabash	Hue.
Brown	Hiku vera.	Cockroaches	Ngarara.
Bury	Muraki.	Cemetery	Papekoo.
Bull	Puaka tamaroa.	Cheek	Kukunne.
Bush	Miro taka-taka.	Dance	Hoko-hoko.
Button	Herreo.	Darkness	Pouri.
Boar	Oru tamaroa.	Day	Raa.
Back	Tua iri.	Death	Mate.
Beard	Vere.	Defeat	Kio.
Bladder	Tana mimi.	Dew	Hau.
Blood	Toto.	Diaper	Hami Kaufa.
Bone	Iri.	Dirty	Go-o-onea.
Breath	Haugu.	Docile	Maugaro.
Buttock	Eve tuki-evo.	Dog	Paibenga.
Bulrush	Naatu.	Drink (water)	Kanuu taa-vai.
Boobies (birds)	Kuia.	Dry	Paka-paka.
Basket	Kete.	Dry, v.	Haka paka-paka.
Calm	Marie.	Dung	Tutai.
Canvas	Hecki keho.	Dwell	Noho.
Cannibal	Kai tangata.	Devil	Atua.
Cat	Gooli.	Dish-cloth	Te maro.
Catch	Kato.	Drinking-cup	Rapa-rapa.
Caught	Roa a.	Dead	Heniati.
Care	Ana.	Ear-ring	Taringa.
Chief	Honui.	Earth	Oone.
Child	Poki iti-iti.	Eat (food)	Kai.
Clean	Maita Kia.	Eat (heartily)	Kai-kai.
Climb	Kabiti.	Evening	Ata-ta.
Cloak	Nua.	Eel	Koiro.
Clothing	Hami.	Ear	Taringa.
Cloud	Rangi tea-tea.	Elbow	Turi rima.
Club (short)	Para.	Eye (or face)	Mata.
Club (dancing)	Ao.	Eye-brow	Hihi.
Club (long)	Ua.	Eye-lash	Veke-veke.
Cocoanut	Niu.	Eye-lid	Tutu Mata.
Comb	Tapani.	Far	Konui.
Cooking place	Heumu.	Feign	Haka kemo.
Correct	Riva mao á.	Female	Tamahiui.
Cow	Puaka tamahiui.	Fire	Abi.

TE PITO TE HENUA, OR EASTER ISLAND.

English	Rapanui	English	Rapanui
Fish	Ika.	Heaven	Rangi.
Fishing	Ika kato omai.	Heavy	Panghi.
Fishing-line	Eaho.	Here	Iuri-iâ.
Fish-hook	Herou.	High	Runga.
Fish-snood	Ekave.	Hot	Vera.
Flea	Koura.	House (hut)	Hare.
Flower	Pua.	Hunger	Maruaki.
Fly	Kakaure.	Hurry	Horo-horan.
Food	Kai.	Hush	Gamu.
Fowl	Moa.	Hat	Hau.
Fork	Manga-manga.	He, she, it	Koia.
Fool	Heva.	Horse	Hoi.
Fray	Tana.	Hen	Eufa.
Fury	Pohi.	Hair	Ranoho
Full	Titi â.	Hand	Rima.
Fancy	Tangi-hangi.	Head	Puoko.
Few	Tae nengo-nengo.	Heart	Mokoikoi.
Face	Mata.	Hip	Tipi.
Fat	Nâko.	Hibiscus	Moana.
Fore-arm	Paonga.	Hill	Otu.
Forehead	Korae.	Heel	Rike.
Finger	Manga-manga.	Infant	Poki porekoiho.
Finger (index)	Rima tubi henna.	Iron-rust	Toto ohio.
Finger (middle)	Roaroa tahanga.	I or me	Kovau.
Finger-ring	Rima tuhi ii hana.	Instep	Peka-peka vae.
Finger (little)	Ko manaroa.	Intestines	Nene-nene.
Foot	Vae.	Ice-plant	Herepo.
For, or to	Ki.	Image	Moai.
Father	Metua.	Jest	Haka reka.
Girl	Poki tamahini.	Joy	Koa.
Give me	Karai-mai.	Kill	Tingai.
Glance	Mata ni.	Knife	Hoe.
Go	Kaho.	Kidney	Makoikoi.
Go away	Rari kau.	Knee	Turi.
God	Atua.	Kelp	Harepepe.
Gold	Tui-tui.	King	Ariiki.
Gold coin	Ohio.	Land	Kaina.
Good	Riva-riva-maitai.	Lantern	Hera parapa.
Grass	Mouku.	Large	Nui.
Grave	Avanga.	Laugh	Ekata.
Great	Nui.	Leaf	Raupa.
Grief	Topa tangi.	Life	Po-o-te tangata.
Gull	Kia-kia.	Light	Maebâ.
Gun	Hango.	Light (weight)	Maruia.
Gave	Eaai.	Lightning	Uira.
Get out	Kahoa.	Little	Iti.
Gourd vine	Hue.	Lonely	Hoko tahi.
Grass (fine)	Turumea.	Long (far)	Kouni roa.
Grass (bunch)	Moku.	Lose, v.	Marere.
Goddess	Kirato.	Limpet (Chiton magnificus)	Hemama.
Good-by	Kauoi.	Leg	Heru.
Greeting	Kakoia.	Lips	Ngutu.
Hail	Rangi.	Liver	Até.
Half	Vaenga.	Lung	Iuanga.
Handkerchief	Rupa.		

Lichen	Kihi-kihi.	Play	Kori.
Leek	Hekekeohe.	Prawn	Ura.
Luck	Heru-ki-to-mea.	Pitch	Piarhioa.
Lobster	Ura.	Population	Heatua.
Man	Tangata.	Puffed	Pupuhi.
Make	Haka.	Pure	Putu.
Male	Tamaroa.	Physilia utriculus	Papa Ki.
Mat	Moenga.	Palm (of hand)	Paraha Rima.
Meet	Pire.	Pancreas	Kiko o te ivi tikâ.
Moon	Mahina.	Penis	Ure.
More	Kina.	Perineum	Vaha takitua.
Morning	Popohanga.	Prepuce	Kiri ure.
Mountain	Mounga.	Pubes	Pukn.
Move	Hakaueke.	Pulse	Ua naiei.
Mud	Oone heke-heka.	Rage	Pohi.
Memory	Manuao.	Rat	Kiora.
Modern	Hou anci.	Red	Mea-mea.
Mamma	U.	Rest	Hakaora.
Moustache	Vere ngutu.	River	Vai tahē.
Mouth	Haha.	Road	Ara.
Muscle	Kiko na-na.	Rock	Maka motu.
Milk-thistle	Poporo-hiva.	Roll, v.	Katuru.
Marshmallow	Mova.	Root	Aka.
Name	Ingoa.	Rope	Huti.
Narrow	Vaka-vaka.	Rain	Ua.
Native	Hoa kona.	Rib	Kava-kava.
Needle	Iri.	Salt	Kava.
New	Hon.	Sand	Oone.
Next	Tetahi.	Sea-urchin	Hetuke.
Night	Po.	See, v.	Kui.
No	Aita.	Servant	Pukuranga.
Now	Anei râ.	Ship	Miro.
Nail (finger)	Mai kuku.	Shirt	Gahu.
Navel	Pito.	Shoe	Kiri vai.
Neck	Ngao.	Shoot, v.	Pakakina.
Nipple	Matañ.	Shooting	Hango pakakina.
Nose	Ihu.	Short	Poto-poto.
Nostril	Poko-poko ihu.	Shoulder	Kapu hivi.
Obsidian	Mahaa.	Silver	Monie.
Oar (paddle)	Matakao.	Sky	Raugi uri-uri.
Obey	Haka-rongo.	Sleep	Hau-uru.
Omitted	Patu.	Slip	Kahinga.
Of	Ka.	Smoke	Au umu.
Paint	Penetuli.	Smoking	Kangan.
Paper	Para-para.	Snail	Pipi.
Path (trail)	Ara.	Soou	Anei ra nei.
Place	Pahu.	Sorrow	Taugi toka-tangi.
Pick	Kaverimai.	Speak	Parau vangana.
Pig	Oru.	Spear	Mataa.
Pine	Koromaki.	Spirit (soul)	Kuhange.
Pipe	Puhi-puhi.	Spring (season)	Vaha hora.
Plaiting	Taura.	Steal (thief)	Toki-toki.
Plant	Mea tupu.	Stand up	Komaru.
Plantation	Kona oka kai.	Star	Hetu.

Stone	Kihi-kihi.	Together	Amogio.
Stone (tool)	Tauki.	Tendon	Na na.
Stone ax	Toke.	Testes	Miripau.
String	Huti.	Thigh	Papa Kona.
Sugar-cane	Toa.	Thumb	Rima metua nea-nea.
Summer	Hora.	Tongue	Arero.
Sun	Raa.	Toe	Manga-mauga vae.
Suspenders	Pena.	Tooth	Niko.
Swallow, v.	Kahoco.	Toe (great)	Manga-manga tumu.
Satchel (valise)	Kete.	To, or for	Ki.
Shell	Pule.	Tea-plant	Ti.
Sit	Noho.	Thread	Taura.
Sit down	Kano.	To fight	Kavava.
Slowly	Koro iti.	To throw away	Parue.
Small	Iti.	To awake	Karu.
Soaked	Ngare-perepe.	To smoke	E ouo.
Stocking	Tokin.	To cough	Etehu.
Stop (halt)	Maroa.	Umbrella	Hemahia.
Stopped	Hakanoho hia.	Under	Iraro.
Stuffed	Mea popo.	Up	Runga.
Sheep	Mamoi.	Urethra	Na nimi.
Sow	Oru tamahine.	Uterus	Henua.
Small univalve	Ngingongi.	Valley	Ava mounga.
Sea-bass	Kodoti.	Vengeance	Kopeka.
Scalp	Kiri puoko.	Vermilion	Ura-ura.
Scrotum	Kiri maripu.	Vessel (water)	Ipu.
Shin	Paka.	Victor	Matatoa.
Shoulder	Kapu hivi.	Vine (fern)	Riku.
Sole (of foot)	Pararaha vae.	Virgin	Niro.
Spine	Tua papa.	Vagina	Takapau.
Spleen	Para.	Vein	Ua.
Stomach	Kopu mau.	Vulva	Kanontu.
Sea-weed	Miritoun.	War	Tana.
Strength	Riri.	Warrior	Tangata Matan.
Shark	Ninki.	Water (fresh)	Vai.
Skin	Kite.	Water (salt)	Vai-kava.
Talk	Paran.	Wave	E.
Tame	Mangaro.	White	Tea-tea.
Taro	Taro.	Who	Korai.
Tattooing	Tâ Konâ.	Whole (all)	Ananakē.
Tenderly	Ko viti.	Wide	Hakarava.
Thief	Toke-toke.	Widow	Hove,
Thin	Paki roki.	Widower	Hovē.
Thirst	Mate vai.	Wife	Na via.
Thunder	Hatu tiri.	Wild	Manu.
Tobacco	Ava-ava.	Wind	Tokeran.
To-morrow	Apo.	Winter	Tonga.
Tree	Miro tupu.	Woman	Via.
Trunk of tree	Tutunna.	Wood	Miro.
Turtle	Honu.	Worm	Koreha.
They	Pouro.	Write	Motu rongo-rongo.
The	Te.	Wet	Rari.
Those	Rana â.	When	Ahea.
Thou	Koe.	We	Matou.

Waist	Kakari manara.	Yes	Aē.
Wrist	Kakau rima.	Youth	Kope tungu-tunga.
White-bait (fish)	Poopo.	You	Koe.
Year	Tau.	Yam	Kape.
Yellow	Pava.		

NUMERALS.

In counting the natives use the fingers of both hands but never the toes.

1 = Ka-tabi.	50 = Ka rima te aangburu.
2 = Ka-rua.	60 = Ka ono te aangburu.
3 = Ka-toru.	70 = Ka hitu te aangburu.
4 = Ka-ha.	80 = Ka raru te aangburu.
5 = Ka-rima.	90 = Ka ira te aangburn.
6 = Ka-ono.	100 = Ka rau.
7 = Ka-hitu.	101 = Ka tabi te rau ma tabi.
8 = Ka-varu.	102 = Ka tabi te rau ma rua.
9 = Ka-iva.	200 = Ka rua te rau.
0 = Aaugburu.	201 = Ka rua te rau ma taki.
10 = Ka tabi te aangburu.	300 = Ka toru te rau.
11 = Ka tabi te aangburu Ka tabi.	301 = Ka toru te rau ma tabi.
12 = Ka tabi te aangburu Ka rua.	400 = Ka ha te rau.
13 = Ka tabi te aangburu Ka toru, etc.	401 = Ka ha te rau ma tabi.
20 = Ka rua te aangburu.	500 = Ka rima te rau, etc.
21 = Ka rua te aangburu Ka tabi.	1,000 = Piere.
22 = Ka rua te aangburu Ka rua.	2,000 = Ka rua te piere.
23 = Ka rua te aangburu Ka toru, etc.	3,000 = Ka toru te piere.
30 = Ka toru te aangburu.	4,000 = Ka ha te piere.
31 = Ka toru te aangburu Ka tabi.	10,000 = Ka mano.
32 = Ka toru te aangburu Ka rua.	100,000 = Ka peka.
33 = Ka toru te aangburu Ka toru, etc.	1,000,000 = Ha ra.
40 = Ka ha te aangburu.	Over one million, mingoi-ngoi.

From 1 to 10 the syllables are pronounced as one word, in a multiple of ten the words are distinctly separated. A record of numbers was kept by stringing pieces of bulrush together.

www.ingramcontent.com/pod-product-compliance
Lightning Source LLC
Chambersburg PA
CBHW020917230426
43666CB00008B/1478